T0146883

Semper Avanti

Semper Avanti

A Story of Love, Determination, and Perseverance

Nancy Bucceri

SEMPER AVANTI
A STORY OF LOVE, DETERMINATION, AND PERSEVERANCE

iUniverse books may be ordered through booksellers or by contacting:

iUniverse
1663 Liberty Drive
Bloomington, IN 47403
www.iuniverse.com
1-800-Authors (1-800-288-4677)

ISBN: 978-1-5320-0381-3 (sc)
ISBN: 978-1-5320-0382-0 (e)

Library of Congress Control Number: 2016916333

Print information available on the last page.

iUniverse rev. date: 12/27/2016

Preface

Life is amazing. And then it's awful. And then it's amazing again. And in between the amazing and the awful it's ordinary, mundane and routine. Breathe in the amazing, hold on through the awful, and relax and exhale during the ordinary. That's just living heartbreaking, soul-healing, amazing, awful, ordinary life. And it's breathtakingly beautiful.

—L. R. Knost, author

It was near midnight on May 12, 2014, when I sat in Terminal E of the Dallas–Fort Worth Airport and first sent out a frantic call for a prayer chain on my Facebook page. I was one week into my new job with a health care information technology firm based out of Texas. I was a remote employee from suburban Philadelphia, so I was supposed to be at the US headquarters in Texas for another three weeks for on-boarding and product training. But a call from the emergency department of a northern Virginia hospital at seven o'clock changed all that. I had just returned to my hotel after grocery shopping for the next week and was about to make my dinner when the phone rang. It was a social worker calling to inform me that my husband was experiencing severe swelling of the brain, which was quickly threatening his life. I spent the next five hours desperately trying to catch a flight back to the East Coast and notifying our children that their father was in critical condition and needed us. Once I had my two flights arranged, I realized how alone and scared I was. Sitting tearfully in the airport terminal awaiting my red-eye flight back east, I needed to send up a flare, and so I turned to my social media.

My husband of almost thirty-two years had been found unconscious in his hotel room in Fairfax, Virginia, at around five thirty in the evening, after he'd failed to show up for a meeting earlier in the day. He had made the three-hour car trip from our home the evening before, after helping our son, Ben, move his belongings out of the freshman dorm at Temple University and back home for the summer.

Ben had one more final exam, but given my trip to Dallas and Bob's travel schedule, we had agreed that Bob would pick up Ben and his belongings on Sunday, drop him home, and then drive to Virginia. Ben would commute back and forth for the last couple of days of school so he could start his new job, take his final, and tie up any loose ends at the campus.

But sometime between his check-in Sunday evening and Monday morning, Bob suffered a massive brain hemorrhage. He was alone in his room, so by the time he was found Monday evening, his only hope for survival was for the doctors to remove a part of his skull so the brain could continue to swell. "But make no mistake," I was told over the phone by the neurosurgeon. "This will not fix anything. The brain damage is done, and we cannot reverse it."

I listened as the doctor explained that should Bob survive, it was possible he could recover some quality of life over a long period of time—or not. The only thing certain was that if they did not remove part of his skull within the next couple of hours, he would die. Because I never heard the doctor say that Bob's chances for recovery were hopeless, I gave the go-ahead for the surgery. I then put the wheels in motion to get me to him and to figure out what to tell our children. There was a reason Bob had been found alive. His time with us was not yet done. I recalled how Bob had lost his father when he was nineteen and how it had devastated him. Because of that, Bob had worked hard all his adult life to take care of himself. He never smoked, drank only moderately, ate a low-fat diet, and exercised regularly. He was determined to be there for his children in their adult years. It was ironic to me that Bob was near death and our Ben was nineteen years old.

My new employer relentlessly sought the quickest path for me back east, and a cousin of Bob's, Ernie, helped me think straight about what to say to our children. Nancy, my good friend next door, got dressed and ready for the three-hour drive to Virginia with Ben, without ever being asked.

By three in the morning Nancy and Ben were at the hospital. Within an hour, our twenty-one-year-old daughter, Julia, arrived from Pittsburgh, painfully aware of her responsibility as decision maker while I was still in the air. It would be another seven hours before I would arrive at the hospital, wearing the same suit I'd had on the day before, but by then at least I knew that Bob had survived the night.

This was an inconceivable turn of events. In an instant our world had changed, and I was completely unprepared for what we were about to live through. I had led a charmed life, married to a great guy who made me laugh and was a wonderful father to our two beautiful children. Bob was an avid outdoorsman, baseball coach, and athlete who took meticulous care of his health. He was a well-respected, self-employed businessman in the electronic payments industry. I had just landed a great new job for a growing company in my field of health care information technology. Our kids were thriving in college. We were looking forward to becoming empty nesters and reigniting the fun of our earlier years. In fact, we had just spent a romantic weekend at the beach before I'd headed to Dallas to start my new job. Life was good.

What follows is the journal I kept from those early days in the hospital in Virginia, through the long months of initial recovery, followed by my own personal strategies for dealing with such a crisis. Writing what was happening proved to be a tremendous source of strength for me as I struggled to cope, take care of Bob, hold the family together, keep my job, and wonder what our future held.

Mine is not a unique story. Each year approximately 795,000 people suffer strokes; stroke is the leading cause of serious long-term disability in the United States.[1] Commercial insurance denials are an ugly part of the picture, with a Government Accountability Office study in 2011 reporting that overall denial rates (not just for brain injury) vary widely across the States but are as high as 40 percent. Only 39 to 59 percent result in reversals, which means that at least 40 percent of the time the family loses that fight. It never occurred to me—as I sat in the Virginia hospital trying to comfort myself that I had done what I could and the rest was up to Bob and God—that our insurance company was going to say it was up to them.

This is not a political story about the state of our health care system and insurance companies. It's about what happened to my husband, what I did, and what we did together to get through it and come out stronger at the other end. But the health care system is part of the story, and so it is in here.

While I was in Virginia, I met a woman called Mary who became my friend. She gave me the phrase that soon became my mantra: *semper avanti*, which means "always forward." Semper avanti became my rallying cry when things seemed dim and I needed something to keep me going. It also became my victory cry as I celebrated each little win. It was a way of reminding myself that I had to keep the momentum going and that things were moving in the right direction. So that is what I have named this story.

---

[1] www.strokecenter.org

Tuesday, May 13, 2014

The doctors described Bob's stroke to me as a hemorrhagic stroke, which means the bleeding originated in the brain, possibly in a weak vessel.

Bob is in critical condition, fighting for his life, and the doctors say that the first seventy-two hours after the surgery are the most critical for survival. They removed the left side of his skull so that his brain could continue to expand and not be further damaged by the pressure. The swelling will peak in this time period. All the doctors I have talked to paint a bleak picture. The best-case scenario is that Bob will survive and will be in recovery for a very long time but will likely require care for the rest of his life.

The stroke severely damaged the left side of his brain, which controls the right-side movement and speech functions. Bob, a man whose early career was as a high-school English teacher, who wrote me daily love letters and sent me Shakespearean sonnets during our courtship, may be left with no language skills. A man who was so conscious of his health that he treated himself to one real ice cream cone a year may require a feeding tube for the rest of his life. He has not been awake enough for us to know whether he hears or feels people who are present. We're assuming he does.

As of Tuesday morning, Bob is still heavily sedated, in critical condition but stable. We're in the seventy-two-hour watch period right now, asking for prayers. If he makes it through that period, Bob will be in intensive care for several weeks and won't move to a rehabilitation hospital for another three or four weeks. That's the best-case scenario.

By evening I make the decision to send Ben back to Pennsylvania with Nancy. I could tell that sitting in the ICU all day was not the best way for him to process and deal with his father's condition. I don't know exactly what is going on in Ben's head, but I know that Bob would want him to finish out the semester and start the job, so that's what I tell Ben to do. He seems relieved. I ask Julia to wait out the seventy-two hours with me, and she seems to want to be here. We agree she will head back to Pittsburgh Friday, assuming progress continues.

I get a hotel within walking distance of the hospital, so we can get a little rest. It is dingy and smells of smoke, and I hate it, but I haven't slept in over thirty-six hours and don't want to be far away. My sister, Barbara, and her oldest, Ally, make the three-hour drive from Salisbury, Maryland, for a brief visit and to offer moral support.

Wednesday, May 14, 2014

This morning over coffee I startle Julia with a sudden explosion of tears while looking at emails on my phone. She thinks it's terrible news, but it's the enormity of what has hit us that suddenly overwhelms me, after the business of getting to Bob and pulling our family together was finally over. In a reversal of roles, daughter comforts mother, and we hug each other while I sob and Julia tells me it's okay.

I pray that what I have done, telling the doctor to do the surgery, was the right thing to do. I am terrified at what Bob's future holds.

Later my friend Kathy calls me and promises to keep close to Ben and check on him while I stay in Virginia. I want to be there for him, and I worry that phone calls won't be enough for me to gauge how he is coping, but I need to stay near Bob.

Later in the day I speak to Liz, a colleague of Bob's. She is the one who insisted that the hotel management open the door to his hotel room Monday night. She told me that at first the hotel management would not even admit that Bob was a guest. But in all the years she had known him, Bob had never missed a meeting or ever been late for one without calling someone. This had been a major planning session for an annual conference that Bob had helped establish and had been leading with a team of colleagues for over a decade. He would not miss such a meeting without a very good reason. Knowing he was expected to be there she had been determined to find out what had happened. She told the management that they would open the door or the police would. When the door was finally opened, there was Bob on the floor, unconscious but still alive. Based on his state of undress, it appeared he had collapsed sometime in the early morning while starting to get ready for the day, but we would never know for sure.

I am anxious to meet Liz and to thank her for her perseverance and for saving my husband's life. She tells me she just hadn't been able to get it out of her head that something was wrong, that she regretted she'd waited a few hours before getting worried enough to act. But I quickly assure her that my gratitude is deep and sincere and that, as far as our family was concerned, there is a special spot in Heaven reserved just for her.

As Julia and I sit quietly and hold vigil by Bob's bed, a priest comes in to meet Bob. I welcome the spiritual support but am taken aback by the jovial nature of the priest. "What a young man. How old is he?" he asks.

"Sixty-two," I tell him.

"Really?" He looks at me carefully. "Wow. I thought maybe you were one of those women that snagged herself a hot-looking young man!"

I am stunned at the inference that I look much older than my husband, who is seven years my senior. "You mean a *cougar*? You think I'm a cougar!"

"Yes, that's it!" he says and laughs. Odd as it may sound, his levity brightens me and makes the day bearable.

Saturday Morning, May 17, 2014

Bob's condition remains stable this morning. The good news is that he has come out of the seventy-two hour period with continued stability, the swelling on the brain is starting to go down a little, and the pressure is as well. But it is very slow. He is still in a medically induced coma to maintain the pressure levels by keeping him still, so he cannot respond to me.

His risks now are more around susceptibility to pneumonia and risk of infection, which are associated more with being in a hospital than with the injury itself. There are also risks associated with changes in the brain pressure, or the possibility of another stroke, but the tests to date do not indicate that. Doctors still don't know what caused the stroke in the first place

There is a measure called the CPP, which indicates pressure change in the brain. The other day Julia and her cousin Kylie were told by the nurses that talking to Bob might stimulate him. The pressure change is an indication of increased brain activity as the number increases. So they started talking to him, and when they saw the numbers go up, it got them really going. They kept talking to him for an hour, telling him all sorts of tales out of school. It lifted our spirits on Thursday.

I keep trying to get a sense of when we will know how much function he has lost, but the neurosurgeon tells me that it will take time, that when recovery starts to happen, improvements in function will be measured in weeks, not in days.

Julia is now back at her summer job in Pittsburgh. Ben finished out his freshman year as planned, started a job at Lowe's, and continues to manage the home front. I instruct him to send me the bills that are coming in so I can pay online. That makes him feel helpful. Neighbors and friends are bringing him a constant stream of food, but he wants to show me he can take care of himself, so he asks me to stop them. Except he recalls the chicken parmesan. the lasagna, the macaroni and cheese all filling up the refrigerator. These women can cook! He changes his mind.

I have moved to an extended-stay hotel in Fairfax for the foreseeable future, so I am less than a mile away from Bob if anything happens. The place is bright and cheerful, and I can resume the new job and work remotely by day, visiting Bob during my lunch break and then again in the evenings. He will not move to Pennsylvania until he is ready for rehab, so we are here for a while, several weeks at least.

Sunday Morning, May 18, 2014
◇◇◇◇

Our friends Kathy and Joe make the three-hour drive from home to visit with us and help me exchange some of my business clothes. It is a huge relief to see friends from home. We visit in Bob's room and then break for dinner before they head back home.

Monday Evening, May 19, 2014
◇◇◇◇

Bob is visited daily by the priest from St. Ambrose parish here in Fairfax. This is the same priest that teased me about being a cougar. His presence gives me some measure of comfort. Bob's condition remains the same. The doctors keep telling me progress will be measured in weeks and months, not in days. The swelling will take a long time to go down, so they continue to keep him heavily sedated. I am trying to be patient. I am now pacing myself, starting back to work by attending product training sessions using WebEx in my hotel.

It actually feels good to be focusing on something else, a welcome relief from the endless hours of watching Bob's motionless body among the machines and waiting for something to happen. I have a normal routine, even though I know it is a temporary normal. There will be lots of new normals before we are done.

The doctor tells me today that the delay in finding Bob did not make any real difference in the outcome of the brain damage. The hemorrhage was big and fast. He had started to dehydrate and experience muscle breakdown, but there was still no indication of what time the hemorrhage had happened. It had stopped as soon as the pressure built up, so no one could have done anything to stop it.

Wednesday Evening, May 21, 2014
◇◇◇◇

Bob's condition remains stable. He is very sensitive to changes, which the nurses can tell from the monitors. They talk as if he is communicating with them: "He doesn't like it when …" or "He likes it when …" and yet there is no audible cue or facial expression from which they get this information. It's a change in numbers. Numbers go up, he doesn't like. Numbers go down, he does like. I visit during a long lunch break while I continue to take my product training remotely from my hotel room.

Thursday Afternoon, May 22, 2014
◇◇◇◇

I am on a break visiting Bob when the doctor rounds. He tells me Bob suffered from hypertension, but I know he was never diagnosed with that and tell him so. I'm even defensive about it. I arrange for him to speak with Bob's primary-care physician back home in Pennsylvania.

In the meantime, they pull back on the sedation during my visit, and Bob startles me by suddenly shifting in the bed. He does it twice! His inner cranial pressure goes up a little too high, so they increase the sedation back to where it was. The other startling thing to me is that he moves on the right side. I tell the doctor, but he doesn't get as excited as I am. It scares me and lifts my spirits all at once. I am taking it as a good sign.

Friday Afternoon, May 23, 2014
◇◇◇◇

I am visiting Bob early because I am moving out of the hotel. A friend and client of Bob's has generously offered me the use of his house for the duration of Bob's stay here, and the house is about twenty minutes from the hospital. The friend will be on vacation and then on a business trip, so I will be alone in the house. I will set up a home office and work remotely through my laptop and cell phone, as I did from the hotel. My employer has been very supportive of the work schedule I have set up. Technically I am not yet entitled to any paid time off or family leave, so maintaining my work schedule is a high priority, and showing value to my new employer is higher still. It is what will sustain us financially.

Bob looks more swollen today because he is so sedentary, so they are giving him diuretics to help flush the fluids out. As he would likely joke, he'll start "peeing like a racehorse." He is holding steady; the brain pressure is well managed, but they will not likely be able to put in the trach tube until he can lie flat during the procedure. So breathing and feeding tubes down his throat continue.

I am heading back home to West Chester this weekend to see Ben, pick up a few things, and just check on the house. Bob will be without visitors for a couple of days, but I know he would understand. I will call in a couple of times to check in with the nurses. My plan is to come back to Virginia Sunday afternoon, so I will only be home for about twenty-four hours.

Saturday Evening, May 24, 2014

Very encouraging news from the ICU nurse today: the ICP monitor came out. This is what monitors the brain pressure, and the decision to remove it means they are no longer concerned that it will fluctuate dangerously. Now they are just monitoring standard vital signs. They have also completely weaned Bob off the anesthetics, so he is starting to be a little more awake. Amber, his nurse, told me he is opening his eyes a little though not yet communicating.

He withdraws from pain stimulation on both sides of his lower extremities. When they pinch him, he draws his limbs in. I am taking this as a good sign but I understand that pain reflexes are the most basic. His right elbow is hyperextended, indicating brain damage to the area controlling the right arm.

Tomorrow or Monday they will be inserting an air tube directly into the trachea through his neck, which will be much more comfortable and safer than the tube in his mouth. They will also put in a percutaneous tube, or PEG, which will provide nutrition, medicine, and fluids directly into his stomach rather than through a feeding tube in his throat. The best-case scenario is that these are temporary. The worse-case scenario is that he will need them permanently, but I am becoming increasingly hopeful that these are temporary measures.

The doctors are continuing the Lasix drip with the goal of having him expel one liter more than what goes in, but that will take time. So not quite "peeing like a racehorse" yet, but as with everything else, he is moving in the right direction.

It felt wonderful to come home, hug my son, catch at least a few friends, and be in my own house and own bed, even if for just a day. There were many small gains today, so I declare it a good one.

Monday Afternoon, May 26, 2014

◇◇◇◇

It is Memorial Day. I spend it with Bob, watching him move and respond; he is opening his eyes a little. But as the nurse said Saturday night, he is not really looking at anything. I am talking to him a lot but also letting him rest. He is not on the anesthetic anymore, but he is not really awake. It worries me, and I hope it is just his body keeping him in natural sleep to continue to heal.

I have been reading up on hemorrhagic stroke. The good news from what I can tell is that the right brain is amazingly able to compensate for the loss of function on the left. The bad news is the recovery can take years—as many as eight. Or more.

I have to shake off my fear of the future and come back to the present. One day at a time. To keep my voice heard I read to Bob from his daily readings of the Magnificat, his daily prayer book, and relay all the important sports news. I am letting him know how much I love him and how his children, family, and friends all love him and are pulling for him.

Tuesday Morning, May 27, 2014

Lucky me, I walk in Bob's room as the doctor is visiting on his rounds. The neck brace is gone, and Bob's gotten a partial shave, so he looks much cleaner and neater with a new goatee. I can't help thinking that he bears an odd resemblance to Walter White, the main character in our favorite TV show, *Breaking Bad,* who transforms himself from mild-mannered high school chemistry teacher to ruthless drug lord, in part with a shaved head and goatee.

Bob's eyes are a little open and blinking, but he still isn't awake enough to really be looking at anything, and he is not responsive to my touch or voice in any way that I can tell. The doctor says that it may take a long time, but it is not necessarily a bad sign. In fact, Bob continues to move in the right direction and will begin weaning off the morphine today.

This is good news, because yesterday I started doing some reading and learned that 50 percent of hemorrhagic stroke patients die in the hospital, and the thirty-day mortality rate is very high, ranging from 40 to 80 percent. Another 60 percent die in the first year. So my spirits were flagging. The doctor confirmed that Bob is not out of trouble yet, but he does continue to progress and that is good news. I will take that.

Wednesday Afternoon, May 28, 2014

Today I bring my lunch to have it with Heisenberg, my new nickname for Bob. It makes me laugh because he does look like Heisenberg, Walter White's street name. The tubes are gone. The trach and PEG are in. The staples in his head are out. Between the bald head, mean scar, and the goatee, he cuts quite an image.

I am reminded that Bob has made big strides since his incident two weeks ago. Yes, the doctors meant it when they said his progress would be measured in weeks, not days. But my friend Peg walked me through the last two weeks from where he was to where he is, and it is all good—at least as good as it can be.

Big strides notwithstanding, he has a long way to go. The neurosurgeon's assessment today revealed Bob's reaction to physical stimulation was on the left side only and he did not respond to any verbal cues. We know the area of the bleed is where the brain controls speech and comprehension, so I guess I should have expected that. Still, I take each day as it comes, and each day of progress provides some ray of hope.

Wednesday Evening, May 28, 2014
◇◇◇◇

Bob is moving from ICU to an intermediate, or step-down, unit within the next couple of hours. The intermediate unit is more intense than a regular med-surg unit in that there are only three patients to every nurse. So he will still be getting good attention, but he no longer requires all the life support and intense monitoring of the ICU.

Thursday Evening, May 29, 2014
◇◇◇◇

I visit Bob for the first time in his new room. He is still unresponsive, seemingly sleeping peacefully and only occasionally moving his left hand or his head for an unknown reason.

I read to him from his Magnificat, give him some of the news I had been saving up, and quietly eat my lunch before heading back to work. It is a cold, rainy day here in Virginia.

Friday Evening, May 30, 2014
◇◇◇◇

My visit to Bob was late today but not uneventful. The good news is that his liver and kidney functions are fine; all organs are functioning okay. He is running a low-grade fever that is being treated with Tylenol. He is on morphine only when needed, and his blood pressure is okay, although it has been fluctuating a bit. And tonight I requested he get a full shave when he is bathed, so we can say goodbye to Heisenberg.

They have started him on physical therapy, and although he cannot yet respond to any verbal cues, they work him through some passive ranges of motion. This weekend I will make it my job to find out more about what they are doing and how often.

My world was rocked a little when the social worker and doctor raised the expectation of discharging him to another facility as early as next week. He is not ready for acute rehab, so under consideration are a long-term acute-care hospital (LTAC) or a skilled nursing facility (SNF, or nursing home). I was not expecting this so soon, and my gut tells me this is not a good sign, especially given that he really has not awakened yet and they still need to aspirate his lungs for him. My job this weekend, as his advocate, will be to try to prepare myself as best I can to make sure he gets what he needs. I want nothing more than for him to be back in West Chester and me to be with our son and sleeping in my own bed, but I don't want to be rushed, either.

I continue to receive outpourings of love, support and concern from friends, family and colleagues. I am so looking forward to the day when Bob can share in this and read all the wonderful messages and cards he has been receiving, because I know he will be truly humbled. In the meantime, it is a great source of strength and hope for me, and I am feeling very blessed.

Saturday Afternoon, May 31, 2014

I am sitting in Bob's room watching him sleep. He is still not really responding to verbal cues, but today I see something that I haven't seen yet. When the nurse pinches his nail bed on his right hand, he moves his right arm. It is a small movement—but a movement just the same. When she pinches his toes, he moves his right arm. It's ever so slightly, but he moves it just the same. The emotion I feel is overwhelming, and I start to cry.

I meet my friend Patty for lunch, who bears gifts from the neighborhood: a cooler full of grilled chicken, homemade soups, cookie bars, and a basket full of candies, books, magazines, and generous gift cards. The bottles of red wine make me smile, as I appreciate how well my former Friday night Bunco party pals know me. The thoughtfulness and generosity move me to tears.

Sunday Afternoon, June 1, 2014
◇◇◇◇

We are on day 21 of this journey. When I come in today, the nurse tells me that Bob opened his eyes on her command and weakly squeezed her finger with his left hand when requested. She has a bright smile on her face. Of course, there is no such response for me so I can give a first-person account. But now that a cold I had been fighting is gone, I am showering him with gentle kisses on his cheeks and forehead and continuing my strategy of squeezing his hand and telling him that I am here, that I have been here, and that I will always be here.

He has not been on pain medication for several days; his blood pressure goes up every once in a while, so they do give him medicine to control that. He looks comfortable, as if he is sleeping peacefully.

I still don't know what lies ahead, but I continue to have hope that someday I will get my husband back. I miss him terribly.

Monday Evening, June 2, 2014
◇◇◇◇

Bob's condition remains status quo, and I have expressed my strong view that he is to go to acute inpatient rehab when he is ready to transfer. I will continue that push. The attending doctor seems with me on this one, so I consider that to be in my favor. The other thing she said today, which helped me feel less as if we are being pushed out, is that he really needs more physical therapy than he can get in an acute-care hospital. And she assures me she is confident in his stability for the three-hour ambulance ride back to Pennsylvania.

Tuesday Afternoon, June 3, 2014

They said progress would be measured in weeks, not days. But today when I arrived, and for the past hour I have been here, Bob has been awake! That was not the case yesterday. But today, in fact, he's been awake so much they moved him to another room with other people so they could keep an eye on him and make sure he didn't try to do anything crazy like remove his trach collar. He keeps doing purposeful movements with his left hand: reaching to touch his mouth, holding onto the oxygen tube, touching his head where the scar is. Does it itch? Is he trying to figure out what the hell happened to him? The nurses tell me he does understand their verbal commands, though he is still not taking mine. Okay, so I make the clichéd wife joke that that's nothing new. I am trying really, really hard not to let my feelings be hurt.

Despite my self-centered disappointment, the idea that the doctor is on my side for acute rehab is such encouraging news, especially since the initial inpatient rehab I want him to go to declined him for not being alert enough. I am mystified to learn that they are working from last Thursday's information! So much has changed since the low point of last Friday. New information is now going to the rehab, and despite the rainy afternoon, this seems to be a sunny day here in Virginia. But I wonder why the vaunted electronic medical records system I read so much about in my work is not proving fruitful in real life. It's still a paper-based world.

Wednesday Evening, June 4, 2014

Today's visit is more like earlier visits with Bob, when he stayed consistently in his sleep state, stirring only slightly to adjust his hand position or to yawn. I ask if anything today represents a setback, and the answer is no. His numbers are still holding, so I remain hopeful, although increasingly resigned to the idea that he may not be sent to an inpatient rehab.. This may mean transferring somewhere else first. But there were no indications of pending transfer, so we are still in a holding pattern.

Thursday Morning, June 5, 2014
◇◇◇◇

"A guy walks into a bar …". I know, it sounds like the opening line to a joke. In my case it begins a love story that started thirty-six years ago—our love story.

It was a hot summer day in 1978 when Bob walked into the bar I was tending in my college town. He chatted me up while he had a beer with his uncle, and the two of them ended up inviting me to go waterskiing. Our first date ended up not on a lake but in a theater watching *Animal House* (the only thing that ever registered us anywhere on the cool meter with our two children). Anyway, we went on that date and have been together ever since.

Today marks the thirty-second anniversary of our wedding. It was the first of the three happiest days of my life. They happened roughly ten and twelve years later with the births of our two beautiful children.

For whatever reason it was that Bob fell in love with me thirty-six years ago, he has always been all in. He asked me to marry him, took those vows and, by God, never looked back.

Years ago, he and I joined with a group to develop a Pre-Cana marriage preparation program, which had been missing from our parish for many years. It is comprised of four segments, or "talks," that are done by married couples on topics that are foundational to every marriage: communication, adjustment, intimacy, and spirituality. I think our time on the Pre-Cana team and Bob's idea of the approach we should take for our intimacy talk illustrates the kind of husband and man he is.

I won't go into all of it here, but we basically talked about intimacy as being physical, emotional, and intellectual. A strong marriage must nurture all three. While I talked about the trials and tribulations that at times conspire against us here, Bob talked about giving ourselves over to God and each other, striving to nurture our intimacy by helping the other be the best person he or she can possibly be.

He came up with what we dubbed "The Big Finish," during which he had the couples turn to each other, hold hands, and look into each other's eyes. He told them—and it was not as corny as it may sound here—that the reflection they saw in the eyes of their partners was the reflection of the best person that they could become through marriage. It rarely left a dry eye in the house. And it was coming from a man who walked the talk.

I am who I am because of the unwavering love, support, and encouragement Bob has given me over the past thirty-two years as my husband. He is the whole package.

So thank you, Bob, for helping me be the best person I could ever hope to be, and happy thirty-second anniversary. I love you.

When I visited Bob today he awakened for about fifteen minutes toward the end of my visit, made eye contact with me, and squeezed my hand. That was a first, and I will indulge myself in the fantasy that he was waiting to spring this on me on our wedding anniversary.

On the gray side, Tuesday seems to have been his most promising day, so it is not likely he will be accepted to acute rehab anytime soon. The attending physician has said he will assess tomorrow and determine next best steps, so I will talk to him then.

I also hope to meet with the physical therapist tomorrow. One of the things no one can tell me, because they don't have a way to really chart it, is how awake he is across the span of a day. I assume physical therapy has some ways of gauging it during their visits. The nurses give me some anecdotal reports that he is awake a couple of hours at a time, but it is nothing official.

So today was not bad, not great. Comme ci, comme ça. Menza menza.

Friday Evening, June 6, 2014
◇◇◇◇

It is a good visit today. The occupational therapist, Susan, spends a lot of time with me, explaining what goes into Bob's therapy and the tag team going on between occupational and physical therapy all week to observe and track his progress. He tolerates about twenty minutes of active therapy at a time, and today I get to observe a session.

I also meet with the new attending physician, who has been following Bob since Wednesday. He is going to prescribe Provigil to see if that will help promote wakefulness, so he can possibly tolerate a little more therapy and track toward the acute rehab sooner rather than later.

We will regroup on Monday and re-engage on the transfer discussion. Everyone is with me on the acute rehab goal, and I think that is why the doctor suggested Provigil, but I am also more resigned to the idea that a skilled nursing facility or long-term acute-care hospital may be the required stepping stone.

Saturday Afternoon, June 7, 2014
◇◇◇◇

There is nothing new to report. Status quo. Sleeping peacefully. I witness some purposeful movement with the left hand while he is in his sleep state, presumably to scratch an itch, but I cannot awaken him.

Sunday Afternoon, June 8, 2014
◇◇◇◇

Bob and I have been sitting together for the past hour, with me showing him the photos I have posted on his blog site and reading some of the comments and guestbook entries. He has been awake the whole time. In fact, the nurse had his TV on when I arrived. He seems to be watching it. I'd love to know whether he really is. At one point he seems to reach for my hand when I hold it out. It is hard to know what he can understand, so I just keep talking as if he does.

Late in the day, a turn of events gives me hope such as I have not yet had. It happens during a visit from his client and friend, Kurt. Apparently the two of them have some Joe Pesci *Goodfellas* shtick they do with each other when they want to make each other laugh. So Kurt says one of the Pesci lines, and the next thing I see is Bob looking at Kurt with a grin, his eyes brightening. And before I know it, his shoulders and chest start shaking. Just like when you laugh. Just like when you freakin' laugh!

So it's not just a good day in Virginia. It's a remarkable day.

Monday Evening, June 9, 2014

We will be relocating home tomorrow! Bob will be traveling by ambulance, of course. He is still not ready for acute rehab so will initially be going to a nursing home in West Chester. Not my first choice, because I remember the place as one we rejected years before when looking for post-acute care for Bob's mother. My current research tells me it has an overall three-star rating from the federal government's Center for Medicare and Medicaid Services (CMS). Apparently there is a bed shortage in the four-star place.

Wednesday Afternoon, June 11, 2014

Bob made the transfer beautifully yesterday. I have been very busy getting acclimated back home, setting up my permanent home office, getting the new care team up to speed, and beginning the process of getting him into acute rehab. We have a renowned hospital right in our backyard that specializes in brain-injury rehabilitation. They say this place works miracles, and I am counting on it.

I have a meeting with his care team tomorrow, so I will have more of an update on the weekend. In the meantime, I am told he had a three-hour session with physical, occupational and speech therapy this morning, so if that holds, it is astounding progress.

It feels so good to be home.

Thursday Evening, June 12, 2014
◇◇◇◇

On the one-month anniversary of Bob's stroke, he is alert, smiling at inside jokes, and trying to talk. It takes me a while to realize he is mouthing actual words, another encouraging sign. He is in there! Bob's barber, Dave, comes in and restores him to his clean-shaven, handsome self. No more beard or remnants of Heisenberg. Bob seems happy with it. I meet with the care team and go over the care plan and set goals. Everyone is on board with the goal of getting Bob ready for acute rehab. He is doing well with therapy but has a mountain to climb. But I am growing more hopeful and less fearful of his future, although I am still jolted awake every morning to the nightmare we are living.

I am informed today that Bob's professional community will be establishing a leadership award in his name this November, with Bob as first recipient. I know he will be deeply touched and humbled by it. He will soon learn his goal for November: acceptance speech in Clearwater, Florida. I reflect on today and think of what my new friend, Mary, kept saying to me all the while I was in Virginia: *semper avanti*, meaning "always forward". It is now that it becomes my new mantra.

Friday Night, June 13, 2014
◇◇◇◇

Friday the 13th, eh? I have a nice long talk with the clinical liaison at the acute rehab, and he is anxious to assess Bob early next week.

Today I remember Bob's glasses and take them in to him. When I hold them up and ask him if he wants them while he watches TV, he gives me a slight nod, yes. Then I tell him he is in the nursing home temporarily so he can get strong enough for acute rehab and eventually come home. Does he want to come home? Yes.

The therapists at the nursing home are with me, and they think he will do so well in acute rehab. As I do, they hope he can get there sooner rather than later. In the meantime they are doing good work with him and I thank them for what they have done so far.

Cousins Ernie and Judy from New York have arrived. It feels so good to see family. I realize now how isolated I was in Virginia and how important the daily calls, texts and emails were. I continue to be thankful for the continued support and prayers.

Sunday, June 15, 2014

Did we see a little of that dry Bucceri humor yesterday? Ernie is a perennial movie fan, and his visit to Bob calls to mind the 1957 movie *The Wings of Eagles*, with John Wayne and Dan Dailey. Ernie asks Bob if he remembers the scene where Dan Dailey comes in and gives John Wayne, who is paralyzed, an inspirational speech that ends with, "You're going to move that toe!"

Ernie then says to Bob, "Well, Bobby, you're going to move that toe!"—at which point Bob keeps his gaze on Ernie and lifts his left leg and repositions it. Ernie just about jumps out of his skin, while Bob just keeps on grinning.

Tuesday, June 17, 2014

Today it has been one week since we came back from Virginia, and what a week it has been! Bob is alert, engaged, and starting to communicate. Every day there has been incremental change. To some degree he has defied the doctors who said progress will be measured in weeks rather than days. I put a sign over his bed that says, "Talk to me!"—and so they do. The staff engages him, and then they tell me what he says. I think it has really made a difference. Ernie and Judy were here for four days, and that made a difference, too, because Bob had lots of engagement. He still has no voice, but I have gotten more practiced at lip reading. I observe a therapy session today, and it is good to see how the therapists work with him.

Wednesday, June 18, 2014

The clinical liaison was out to see Bob and considers him to be an excellent candidate for their acute rehab program and transfer, but it still needs to go through the insurance company for approval. He told me today he is pulling in the rehab neurologist to add to his case and collecting all the medical information and input from the therapists who have worked with Bob to date. He is optimistic, but he tells me brain injuries can be tricky when it comes to insurance, so it is not a done deal.

In the meantime, this morning I give Bob a shave with his new electric shaver. I do okay, and he approves, but I tell him that by the time I get really good at giving him a close shave he will be doing it himself again.

By afternoon I am back in the Washington, DC, area, this time on a short business trip. I will return Friday. I have passed the shaving baton to Ben for the time being.

Friday, June 20, 2014

I receive the devastating news that the referral for rehab has been denied by the insurance company. It is now being appealed. If the denial stands, he will continue to get care at the nursing home, and the rehab will continue to follow up and try again in a week or two. Red flags keep going off in my head, but I am counting on logic and reason to win the day.

Saturday Morning, June 21, 2014

Today was a rough, rough morning for Bob. He fell out of bed early this morning while attempting to come see me. He received a full assessment and seems to be okay, and now there is a nurse's aide assigned one on one with him. They have taken some additional measures to protect him, but since it is illegal for a nursing home to restrain a resident (they are not considered patients but residents, I am told) putting an alarm on the bed and chair with a pad on the floor is about all they can do. I ask why this was not done when he was first admitted but receive no answer.

This episode highlights the inadequacy of a standard nursing home to handle the rehabilitation of a person like Bob. I leave a message with the acute rehab liaison, hoping that the nursing home's inability to protect Bob and his fragile head is additional evidence that he needs to be moved to acute rehab, where they have more experience with people like Bob. Acute rehab hospitals have leeway in providing dignified restraints to keep a person with no protective skull from further damaging his brain.

I am sitting by Bob's side, letting him sleep. We spend about a half hour outside looking at the morning papers, me drinking my Wawa coffee and Bob enjoying some fresh air.

I am not in a good place today. I am angry, sad, frightened, and frustrated. I have not yet gotten sufficient assurance that the fall did not do further damage. There is no doctor here, let alone a neurologist. I don't understand a health system that goes to extraordinary measures to save a man's life and then consigns him to a nursing home that is not capable of providing the necessary, proper care.

Saturday Night, June 21, 2014

His vital signs have been checked every thirty minutes, and Bob has been as alert and responsive as he was prior to the fall, so thank God he is fine. It is still very, very scary. Registered nurses attend to him, but it is an aide who has been sitting with him. I am with him again and will probably stay the night.

I understand that nursing homes are residences and not hospitals. The laws restricting restraints stem from abusive practices used by some to keep costs down. I understand that there is indignity in restraints and that people have "a right to fall," as the nursing home's nurse manager informed me. I get that. We live with risk every day, whether we are young, old, healthy, or infirm. But what I don't get is why our health system will go to the trouble to remove part of a man's skull to save his life but then put him in harm's way in an inadequate facility before that protective skull piece can be put back. One minor blow to the left side of his head could kill him or, worse, traumatize the brain beyond its ability to repair.

Sunday, June 22, 2014

Today is the calm after yesterday's storm. Bob and I spend a good six hours outside; it is such a gorgeous day. By late afternoon it becomes almost a party, with a steady stream of visitors. It is so nice to sit at a table under an umbrella and just visit with each other. At one point Bob is overwhelmed by the attention and becomes emotional. Holding back tears and still without a voice, he tells us, "I want to get better!" I assure him he *is* getting better and that patience and perseverance will win the day.

I cannot read every sentence coming out of his lips, but he is clearly communicating a lot today. He tells the aides he wants to wear pants, not shorts. Last week you had to say, "Pants?" and wait for the nod yes, and then go to "Shorts?" if you didn't get the nod. He is now nodding side to side to indicate no, while last week he could only nod up and down for yes. While I pay some of the bills, I ask him whether I should keep paying some of his business subscriptions every month or suspend them until he has recuperated. He responds by forming the sentence, "Suspend them until I am recuperated," with his lips.

The communication challenge is mostly in our inability to read his lips and know what he is saying. There are many times when he clearly has something to share during conversations, but we are not always able to make it out. I have no idea what I should say at a time like that, so I tell him the truth, that I am sorry we are not able to understand him all the time, but he should be patient, keep trying, and it will come.

So the day is a good one, but it has been an upsetting weekend for him for two reasons: he experienced an extremely dangerous fall that could have been devastating, and the enormity of what happened to him is still hitting him. I can't imagine what he is going through. What must it be like to express a perfectly clear thought, only to have your wife and friends look at you blankly? What must it be like to think you can get out of bed and walk, only to find yourself crashing to the floor?

Monday, June 23, 2014

Bob will soon be on his way to one of our region's best academic medical centers so they can monitor him for a day or two and run a few CAT scans to rule out any possibility of new bleeding as a result of Saturday's fall. Why? Because the nursing home's therapists noted Bob was not sitting up as straight today. He was leaning heavily, and he could not tolerate the same level of therapy they had given him Friday. I found out they'd had him standing on Friday, but he could not do it today. While it could be the normal good-day/bad-day scenario, the doctor decided it would be best to rule out the possibility of a new bleed. So we are sent off to our local hospital's emergency department for a CAT scan.

In the meantime, the clinical liaison at the rehab informs me that the insurance company denied Bob again, this time after a peer-to-peer review with a behavioral neurologist and the health plan's medical director. I am stunned, and I ask why. He pauses, hesitating to tell me the devastating news. "Frankly," he says, "they just don't think he can get any better. I am so sorry." After I hang up, I sob alone in the car before drying my eyes, putting a smile on my face, and meeting up with my husband. Semper avanti.

The emergency department visit is a waste of time. Without a baseline CAT scan from the initial event in Virginia, it is impossible to tell whether a new bleed has occurred. No one thought of that before sending Bob off in an ambulance. Additionally, our local hospital has no neurosurgeon, despite all the billboards around town advertising the new brain center. After six hours in a gurney in Corridor H, it's off to the city he must go.

I can't help but think about the industry I work in and all the trade news I read about the money being spent on health information technology. The United States government has paid over $30 billion to hospitals and doctors to adopt electronic health-record systems, which are required to communicate and share clinical information from one health system to another. I realize in hindsight the Virginia hospital should have given me a disk with the last CAT scan as a baseline to give his new care team in Pennsylvania. So much for that.

While my friend Kathy and I are standing next to Bob on his gurney in the hallway under the big cardboard H, I notice that his oxygen tube is not connected to his oxygen tank. I make several attempts to get someone to take notice and connect the tube. Each time I get a person to stop, he or she looks the situation over for a few seconds and then asks me what the oxygen setting should be. I say I don't know. Invariably the person shrugs an *Oh well* and walks away. A physician assistant stops by, presumably to do an assessment. I am asked a series of questions, all of which

I am able to answer. I am then asked what medications Bob is on. I tell them he has a complete medication list that is part of his transfer documentation from the nursing home. "Where is it?" I am asked. "Down there at the nurse's station," I say, pointing about one hundred feet away. She turns in the direction my finger is pointing and then back to me to say, "That's okay; never mind," and walks away.

Wednesday, June 25, 2014

Many wheels are in motion to get Bob into the acute rehab where he belongs. The clinical assessment out of the academic medical center is that he is stable, has not suffered any new bleeding, and is ready for acute rehab whereby he can get more than three hours of therapy a day. The team in the city has been providing therapy and is ordering a barium test, the first step in weaning him off the feeding tube. This will test his ability to swallow food. It was actually the idea of the speech therapist at the nursing home after she successfully introduced a little bit of food the Friday before. The speech pathologist at the academic hospital thought it was a great idea. She is also ordering an assessment of the trach because his breathing has been excellent. This hospital team has been fully apprised of the insurance company's denial and is in agreement that it is "ass". This is Ben's way of saying it, not mine, but in my anger and frustration it seems fitting. The hospital care team, nursing home team, and the acute rehab are galvanized with me to build a clinical case for overturning the denials.

I have also turned to my company's human resources director, who has gone to our broker to see whether there is any opportunity to influence the insurance company from that direction.

The nursing home staff share with me what Bob has been getting in physical and occupational therapy: simple grooming, bed-chair transfer, chair positioning, standing frame, sitting balance, hand-eye coordination, visual scanning, one-step instruction, gentle stretching, out-of-bed tolerance, and bed mobility. For speech therapy, he tolerates the speaking valve for twenty-one minutes at a time, and he is reading and practicing holding a pen. He is on a daily three-hour schedule.

Yes, Ben, the insurance company is "ass."

Saturday, June 28, 2014

Although I have the care teams on my side, the insurance company has now denied and denied again the academic hospital's referral to acute rehab. So this makes two separate attempts and two separate appeals by two separate health care organizations that have been lost. I contact the insurance company directly and try to talk to someone, so I can understand what they need for approval. The denial letter even invited me to do so! I am told the reason for the denial is that the clinical information is inefficient to convince them Bob can tolerate fifteen hours of therapy a week.

It makes no sense. Everyone who has seen and worked with Bob says he can tolerate three hours a day, and the nursing home therapists attest that he already is. They insist to me they are giving this information to the insurance company. I can't figure out where the breakdown is in communication.

Try as I might, I am completely ineffective in intervening on Bob's behalf. It is like spitting into the wind. Every facility and every floor in every facility assigns a new social worker when the patient moves. I am constantly chasing people through a labyrinth of social workers, nurses, and clinical liaisons and never catching the right person at the right time in the decision process. I am always one step behind.

A urinary tract infection delays Bob's discharge. It is not lost on me that this whole hospitalization would have been avoided if the hospital in Virginia had included the last CAT scan with Bob's transfer records. He will remain at the academic hospital probably until Monday and then likely move back to the nursing home. In my mind he has had a setback, losing a full week of therapy. I will continue to fight for acute rehab, but I don't expect to win anytime soon. In the meantime, I follow the news stories about our political leaders' and the media's preoccupation with free birth control as the national priority for health care. I am facing an insurance company denying the care that is covered under our policy based on criteria that he is already meeting but it is ignoring. The absurdity of it all turns my stomach.

Monday, June 30, 2014

Bob is back at the nursing home, hopefully scheduled to get back into his therapy program tomorrow.

The battle to get him into the acute rehab continues. The bad news is that the insurance company denied the academic hospital even after a peer review. The documented notes in Bob's chart from the hospital physiatrist said Bob "did not fully cooperate" during the neurological exam. Despite the facts that this inconsistency in participation is normal in brain-injury patients and that he was sick with a bladder infection, it was enough to justify the denial. I call the neurologist to understand what the hell has just happened and to sarcastically thank him for throwing my husband under a bus. He is kind and lets me vent. He assures me the phrase is a standard clinical term and does not indicate a reversal in the team's recommendation for acute rehab. He tells me he is sorry for the insurance company's stance.

The good news is that Bob will get three hours of therapy a day at the nursing home. The bad news is they cannot give Bob the level of therapy he needs, and they are not equipped to protect and care for a brain-injury patient in the manner he requires. I have decided to hire a patient advocacy firm recommended by our family attorney. He tells me they are reputed to have a high degree of success overturning this particular insurance company's decisions on appeal, so I figure it is worth a shot.

I am very concerned about the nursing home's inability to keep Bob safe from further falls. I know now that acute rehabs can use restraints because they fall under the laws governing acute-care hospitals. The same laws do not govern a sub-acute facility, which is what the nursing home is. I keep raising that as a safety issue, and they all nod their heads in agreement with me, but it doesn't change a thing.

Despite all this and the urinary tract infection, Bob is still going in the right direction. I did see his right arm move slightly the other day while he was dozing, though the doctor said it could just be reflex. I told the same doctor about when we were watching the Phillies game and how Bob could answer detailed questions I had about the players, though he was still mouthing the words without sound. That seemed to catch the doctor's attention.

Wednesday, July 2, 2014

Last night I sat next to Bob as he read a section of our daily newspaper for the first time since May 12. Images of the final scene from Mel Brook's comedy *Young Frankenstein* popped into my head. You know, Peter Boyle's monster with his misshapen head and zipper-neck scar sitting in bed reading the Wall Street Journal, much to the amazement of Madeline Kahn's bride. Anyway, it was a rare moment of levity yesterday as it was confirmed for me once again that Bob is in there.

I am riding a roller coaster of devastation and euphoria as Bob's progress continues but keeps going unnoticed by the insurance company. Just as I am setting in motion an appeals process with my newly hired patient advocate, I receive a call at the end of my workday from the nursing home business office. They inform me that Bob will be discharged in nine days. In a cheerful voice I hear he is welcome to stay under private pay. My heart stops. Panic threatens to overtake me. But then something noticeable happens to me. Just as quickly as the panic rushed in, a strong sense of calm settles over me. It is unlike any calm I have ever experienced before. It felt supernatural. Is this the hand of God calming me down when I feel I have reached the final straw?

At a subsequent meeting with the nursing home team, they imply that Bob could still be approved for acute rehab. In fact, from their perspective it appears that the insurance company may be looking for information to support such an approval.

So the nursing home team is galvanized to get him approved. Everyone is convinced of Bob's potential, based on progress to date, but the fact that the insurance company has played hardball so far has made us all understandably paranoid.

To that end, I redirect the patient advocate to hold on the appeal and work with the nursing home team to ensure we get as much clarity as we can from the insurance company on what we need to gain approval. Then we can put forward the best possible referral. I ask her to work with both the nursing home and the rehab physicians to ensure we are all on the same page and make as cogent an evidence-based, clinically sound argument as possible. Research confirms that a person with strong cognitive skills and severely weakened motor skills is an excellent candidate for acute rehab. Bob is such a candidate, and everyone will see it if we do this right, I keep telling myself.

I then go back upstairs to Bob and tell him as I point my finger in his direction, "Look, mister!" No matter how tired he gets, for the next nine days he has to work hard with the therapists. His future is riding on it. He nods in recognition.

Just to make sure that progress continues, the speech therapist decides to introduce a food diet tomorrow, and at my insistence, the nurse is taking steps to get him off the trach. This was never addressed during the hospital stay, despite my requests, because the hospital team did not want to remove a tube it had not placed. I tell them it was done in Virginia so someone has to do it! It made no impression.

Bob is also being set up with a portable oxygen device so he can more easily receive guests outside of his dreary room. He is getting more time on the speaking valve, though not unsupervised yet. His fever has been gone for several days, and he feels better. Semper avanti.

Thursday, July 3, 2014

I receive a call in the early afternoon that quite literally rocks my world—Bob walked eight feet! I don't even understand at first and make the therapist explain what she means. When I hang up I look to the heavens and start to laugh out loud. I tell myself the insurance company can't possibly ignore that. Semper avanti.

Saturday, July 5, 2014

Thursday's euphoria must have exhausted me because yesterday I felt as if I'd been run over by a truck. Thank God it was a holiday. It was a good day with Bob, spent outdoors in the afternoon as the weather cleared. While he and I were alone for a while, we got on the topic of what had happened on May 12 and what had followed.

Bob knew he had had a stroke, and he knew it had happened in Virginia and he had been in the hospital there. What he didn't know were all the details. He didn't know his children had been with him when he came out of surgery and that by eleven o'clock that Tuesday morning his "crew" had been in full force. That's what he always says when the children are home and the four of us are together: "I'm with my crew." He didn't know that Nancy had been there to support our children until I could get there. He learned about all the people that had visited him in Virginia. He learned about the steady stream of phone calls from family, friends, and colleagues across the country. I showed him the website again and the volume of prayers and well wishes. He didn't remember that I had been there holding his hand and talking to him every day. I told him the doctors had said he wouldn't remember, but I did it anyway because I believed he'd know it while I was there and it would help him get stronger. I told him I believed those things, and he nodded that he did too.

It was emotional for him. I told him I hoped it was okay that I had told him everything and asked if it was overwhelming. He nodded to say that it was but told me it helped him put everything in perspective. He'd had no idea that so many people cared so much. Ben came for his daily visit after work, and we were able to lighten things up with humor.

Today Bob's brother, Ben, arrives from California to the good news about Bob's first steps. He is here for an extended stay, to give Bob the attention and support he needs as Bob gets more and more engaged in his rehab work and I continue to work my new job. We are now Ben, Ben, and Nancy living at the house. Darryl, Darryl, and Larry from the old *Newhart* TV show comes to mind, and it makes me laugh. I will call them Ben the Elder and Ben the Younger.

Around dinnertime we go back up to his room and are greeted by his dinner tray. So ensues the tug-of-war. "Eat your soup," I command.

"No," he forms with his lips.

"Please eat your soup," I beg.

"It's horrible," I read him saying.

I taste the salty soup. "It's not that bad!" I lie. "Here, Ben will eat some. See? It's fine. Now eat it," I say as I ignore the grimaces from our son.

"This food sucks," I make out. I ask the nurse whether there is something else. She brings tomato soup made with a thickener.

"Okay, here—you like tomato soup," I say as I push it toward him.

"It has lumps," he says silently.

"Those are pieces of tomato," I lie.

"They're white," he says as he clearly identifies the lumps of thickener.

We confirm yet again that Bob is indeed in there—and stubborn, as usual. He cannot be cajoled into doing anything he does not want to do. But his problem with the food is valid so from now on we will try pureed food from home. Semper avanti.

Monday, July 6, 2014

Ben the Elder and I watch Bob walk again during his physical therapy session. He goes about six feet and then stands at the standing frame for about six minutes. He is working so very hard. It is clearly a huge struggle. We talk again about the importance of eating the food he gets. I keep reminding him it is his ticket off the feeding tube, so he tells me he ate his three meals yesterday. He now has a refrigerator full of homemade and Progresso pureed soups, rice, chocolate puddings, and pureed peaches. He likes all those things, so we'll try to keep him stocked and figure out new things so he does not have to eat institution food for dinner.

It is hard to fathom that the insurance company will deny him admission to rehab again, but in the event they do, I will be using every avenue: the patient advocate to help with the formal appeal process, Pennsylvania legislators, the insurance commission and possibly attorneys.

Today it is beautiful out but too hot, so we stay in and start watching episodes of *House of Cards* from his iPad. Semper avanti.

Wednesday, July 8, 2014

Bob's progress continues. He continues to get all three therapies, including walking (eighteen feet yesterday, six feet at a time), though today Ben the Elder reports that Bob is experiencing abdominal pain. An x-ray and lab work have been ordered to see if something unseen is going on with the feeding tube. Hopefully it is just irritation and sore muscles from all the therapy work.

On Sunday we were able to hear more of Bob's speech. He spent forty-one minutes on the speaking valve, but even when it was off it was easier to hear his whispers in a quieter room. The therapist wanted him to say something to me, so I decided that, since he had been asleep on June 5, he owed me a "Happy Anniversary." I got it, thank you very much.

Having Bob's brother here is a blessing. This is true brotherly love, to come across country by train for an extended stay when you have your own health issues and could be home enjoying your grandchildren. Ben the Elder has spent the last two days in therapy with Bob, sitting on a rolling stool ahead of him at the parallel bars prodding and pushing him with commands like "Bigger step— come on!" I told Bob that he might not have been a United States Marine going into this, but his brother will make him one before he gets out.

Julia arrived home this evening and will stay until Friday. She didn't wait until morning; she and I headed over right after dinner. He was so happy to see her and get a big kiss. We visited for only about forty-five minutes, and I think he wanted us to stay longer, but I have caught a cold, so I am trying to get to bed early these days.

I have no news on the appeal process other than to say we are going ahead with it. We are continuing to work with the nursing home to document the steady progress and gains that warrant continued care and therapy. Semper avanti.

Friday, July 11, 2014

I have been spending my discretionary time these last two days filing a formal member appeal with the insurance company, a formal complaint against them with the Insurance Commission of Pennsylvania, and finally, hiring attorneys. How did we get here? The insurance company's case manager gave the nursing home staff the impression everything was in order for authorization to acute rehab, but yet another medical director denied the referral. Again, they say there was not enough documentation to support the move. So the nursing home people turned the place inside out today to try to give the insurance company what it wants, but I have no illusions that it will change anything. The part I resent is that it has taken away my time for actually visiting my husband. My one-hour visit after work does not satisfy either of us, but we both know it has to be this way right now. Thank God for his brother, Ben, and for our children. Last night Bob told me how grateful he is for the support system, how his brother has been so helpful, and how our children are such a blessing to him.

His progress continues. Last night I could hear his whisper and occasionally heard voice sounds. Tonight not so much, but he was very talkative and engaged with Ben the Younger and me during our after-dinner visit. But the progress is slow. Painfully slow. He is fidgety. He wants to be up and moving. He is tired of sitting around. He says three hours of therapy is not enough anymore. He wants to come home. He wants to go fishing. He wants to eat hot dogs. And he doesn't even really like hot dogs.

My sister wrote and advised us that we are fighting a nasty dragon. She knows what she is talking about, having fought her own dragon all her life. She survived polio as a child but lives with a disability. We can get angry. We can feel sad. We can get overwhelmed. But in the end, we shall prevail. And we need to keep smiling. I make sure I smile at every therapist, every aide, every nurse, every social worker, and thank them for their kind care.

I am tired tonight, not feeling particularly witty, not wanting to put up a good front. All I want—all I want in this whole wide world—is for one medical director at the insurance company to be a human being for five minutes and realize that he or she is toying with another human being's life. Another human being's family. A human life that the insurance company allowed the doctors to save but now won't allow his best chance for getting his life back.

Monday, July 14, 2014

Today comes the news that not only has the insurance company persisted in its denial of acute rehabilitation for Bob, it has determined his post-acute coverage at the nursing home has ended. They will no longer pay for his room and board or his rehabilitative therapy. He is on his own. They are using the convalescence benefit in our policy as the justification for ending coverage. But none of the experts who have been working with or advocating for Bob define his last twenty-five days as convalescent care. And insurance medical directors I know have said the same. Now the insurance company will not accept any new documentation that the nursing home assembled on Friday regarding its request last week to better substantiate their most recent referral. Now that we have filed an appeal about the last referral, the insurance company is shutting down all further attempts to provide evidence that acute rehab is appropriate, reasonable, and warranted.

I am struck by an article in the newspaper this morning about a couple that just won a long and difficult battle with Nationwide over a car repair that was done in 1996. The crux of it: Nationwide spent $3 million in legal fees to get out of paying $25,000 to replace the Jeep. In that case, no lives were lost or ruined, but it was Nationwide's willingness to put a family on the road in a car that was structurally unsound that was at the heart of the lawsuit. That and not disclosing to the family that the original assessment by the repair shop totaled the car.

In our case, it is Bob's life and our family that are at stake. It occurs to me that the clinical criteria is just an excuse, the documentation could be perfect and it would still be ignored because the business model is to simply deny until the family either goes away or the company is forced to pay. My thoughts sarcastically go to a new tag line for the insurance company: "Don't mess with us. We will outlast you."

The attorneys have accelerated their efforts to get a demand letter to the insurance company because we are now in a private-pay situation and will soon begin burning through money. I told the attorneys I don't want to stop therapy and wait this out because of the devastating effect that would have on Bob's morale, if nothing else. They have not yet advised me that this will hurt our chances of getting the insurance company to back down. I can't imagine letting Bob just sit around for weeks, maybe months, if they do. What if this takes years?

On the contrary, Bob is getting very aggressive and wants to get moving. He actually forced a situation today that allowed him to use the bathroom. He insisted on using the toilet, and so two aides and Ben the Elder actually helped get him into the bathroom. When I heard of this later in the afternoon, I called the head of rehab at the nursing home and asked her whether one of his therapies could focus on the use of a commode. She agreed to put that as a new goal, and we have also agreed to increase physical and occupational therapies to six days a week.

Bob knows the insurance company has been a roadblock, but I do not permit it to be a focus of conversation. That is not his fight, so he is not to worry about it. That is my fight. His fight is to focus on doing his rehab so he can come home. Will the attorneys tell me to stop while they try to force the issue with the demand letter? I pray not. God, I pray not.

In the meantime, we continue to enjoy dinners from neighbors and friends who are helping those of us at home to stay focused and well nourished. The meals are delicious. I can't thank all the people enough. The support system, and I don't just mean the meals, is nothing short of amazing. I know that without it I would not be able to cope with half of this. Not only are we being cared for, but Bob and I have also been visited by new and old friends. Bob even got a shave and haircut this morning. He's decided to keep the new look and just had his beard and mustache trimmed. I guess a little bit of Heisenberg has come back.

Bob continues to show remarkable resolve to regain his mobility. Later this week he will be going for an MRI of his brain so the hospital neurosurgeon can assess where he is with the healing process, in anticipation of replacing the skull flap. The date for that has yet to be determined. He will also get a procedure this week to reduce the trach. He continues to move to a food diet. Despite the insurance company's attempts to destroy him and our family, we continue to press forward.

Wednesday, July 16, 2014

Today was a big visiting day, from what I could tell with all the text messages coming my way while I was at work. There was a steady stream of friends from two o'clock until just before I arrived at quarter after seven. He loved the visits and the encouragement from all who visited him. It helped reaffirm for me that we are not wrong. What Bob needs is both reasonable and justified, because with aggressive therapy, he will get better. Semper avanti.

Thursday, July 17, 2014

I arrive at the nursing home at seven o'clock this morning for an early morning doctor's appointment, only to have the process of getting Bob dressed take so long that the van driver leaves, and we have to reschedule for ten o'clock. Worse than that, a woman smiles at me and Bob while we're waiting for the transfer van and asks me, "Is that your son?" *Aargh*. And on top of that, it will cost me a half day off work. But this appointment is important because it is about removing the trach. And I get extra time with B.

At the doctor's office, Bob and I are not sure what to expect other than a consult. We do not expect to leave without the trach—but before we know it, the trach is out and Bob is free to go. Big, big day! Now that the trach is out, he has a lot to say. It's still a little hard to hear him, but hear him we can. For the first time in over two months, we have a husband-wife conversation.

Despite my intentions, therapy has stopped until we can either get Bob where he belongs or I can negotiate a private pay rate that is not $1,500 a day.

The demand letter should go out today. I am praying that this is resolved soon. Bob tells me he knows the insurance company thinks this is a waste of money. We know differently.

Friday, July 18, 2014

The insurance company denies my member appeal and upholds its position after receiving the demand letter from the attorney today. The nursing home will not negotiate on the daily rate, insisting on its private-pay rate, which is four times higher than what the insurance company is paying. We are expected to pay $1,750 a day versus the $420 a day the multimillion-dollar insurance company has been paying. I suddenly see how the system works: drain the patient's savings and push him into Medicaid, so the taxpayers can pay. It is very interesting when you think about it. The system really is designed to destroy families, drive them into poverty, and then make them dependent on the government.

In the meantime, Bob sits up straight without assistance and without a chair back for thirty minutes and does handheld-weight exercises with his left hand. He eats a peanut butter-and-jelly sandwich for lunch and explains to his brother and me what his speech therapist has told him earlier in the day: his brain is sending the appropriate messages to his hand, for example, but the hand is not yet picking up the messages. He also explains to us that his best speech therapy now is simply to talk, and so he does. For two hours.

This is where my brain has so much trouble making sense of all this: it absolutely defies logic that the insurance company would deny a person who is so clearly meeting the standard criteria for acute rehab. There is no logic to it, and yet there is every possibility that they will never back down.

Back to the real goal. Bob wants to come home. What do I need besides a wheelchair ramp, a wheelchair, and a stair lift? I need Bob to be able to do some things on his own or with only some assistance from me. I am not sure how far away from that we are, but I am going to try to find out.

In the meantime, the lawyer is preparing for legal action and the insurance commission response to the complaint is still pending. But I am not optimistic that anything will come of it soon. Semper avanti.

Sunday, July 20, 2014

It was a good day today. Bob and I did ninety minutes of physical therapy together in the therapy room. Yesterday I was certified to help Bob with a standing exercise that is a key requirement for getting back the use of his right leg. Despite its many steps, it is beautiful in its simplicity: we bring the wheelchair up to a wall with a guide rail, properly placing Bob's feet. With my hand grabbing his waistline, and me bracing under his weak arm and blocking his right knee with my leg, and his left hand holding onto the guide rail, he stands up and just stays there, straight and tall. That's it. We did a series of six with Bob standing straight and tall each time, and each time requiring less work from me. We did six 60-second stands, each one getting easier. Our goal for the week is to get to five minutes without having to sit, but the therapist said that it is more important to have good form than to log a lot of time. Doing this is a lot more work than the standing frame, which has a harness that helps support him. The work, says Bob, is not the exertion of standing. It is the concentration of putting all the moves together and concentrating on the posture. Listen to that: the concentration of putting all the moves together needed to just stand up. This is what he is facing.

We also did arm curls and leg lifts using dumbbells and wraparound weights. We did abdominal exercises. It was fun, and it felt good to be doing something so important together.

Yesterday we had our first spat in over two months. "Who are you calling cheap?" It felt great to be standing in front of each other, looking each other in the eye and talking. But somehow we got on the subject of how he thinks I am tight with money. "Oh yeah? And who has three quarters of the closet?" I demand.

"Where are you going with this?" he asked.

"I'm not cheap. You waste money. You must have nine million T-shirts! And one jacket for when it's forty degrees and sunny, another one for when it's forty degrees and cloudy. And the shoes …" We had a lot of fun making the therapists laugh, and before we knew it Bob had stood for fifteen minutes in the standing frame.

By the way, *cheap*, my ass. It's called *frugal*.

Monday, July 21, 2014

"Today was a productive day," said Bob. Let us count the ways: (1) He was visited by his business partner and friend, Art, who came not only to see him but to bring him some project work. (2) He walked twenty-six feet in one trip. Yep, twenty-six feet. And then right after that, he did another ten feet. These are assisted walks, with a therapist helping on each side with balance and manipulating the right foot for him, but they are walks just the same. (3) He corrected my grammar for the second time in two days. (4) He stood at the handrail, with me giving minimal support, for over five minutes. (5) He ate potato salad, a "chopped" Italian hoagie on a soft roll, orange sherbet, ground beef, and a brownie. (6) He had a cup of Wawa's Kona coffee with light cream. This was my treat. I couldn't let his first cup of coffee be anything else. He has officially moved to soft solid food. I have a feeling he will never allow me to serve him pureed food again.

On the insurance battle, I learned the demand letter, was a waste of time. We are moving to an expedited external appeal. This is the administrative process we learned we must exhaust before taking legal action. As the Wicked Witch of the West once said, "Patience … pa-a-atience!" But my God, I hope this works. And if the external appeal fails, I will want the attorney to move quickly. The clinical liaison from the rehab came by for another assessment today and was once again bowled over by Bob's progress. He is as dumbfounded about the insurance company as everyone else. It is comforting to hear that he believes Bob is getting good therapy at the nursing home, which calms my fears that Bob is losing time or not progressing well enough. So we both still feel a sense of urgency about getting him into acute rehab but are not panicked that he is losing ground.

I think we are heading into a good week. And just in time, because Wednesday is Bob's birthday. I see a Carlino's lasagna in his future … semper avanti.

Tuesday, July 22, 2014

The highlight of Bob's therapy was that he walked forty feet in one stretch today. The right leg muscles are reportedly starting to twitch, which the therapists say is a good sign. Someone brings Bob a delicious bread pudding from the diner across the street, which Bob saves to share with me, remembering my love of bread pudding. There is an onslaught of visitors, including my Aunt Judie and Uncle Earl, who have made an almost-four-hour drive from New Rochelle, NY, and several sets of neighbors and business friends. By the time I arrive in the evening, I notice his voice is consistently hoarse, less than a whisper. Birthday tomorrow.

Wednesday, July 23, 2014

Happy birthday to my B! For dinner we have lasagna and broccoli rabe from our favorite Italian market and, of course, cake and ice cream. He eats like a horse.

I am struck tonight by how happy we all are and how I feel as if it is the best birthday ever. How can that be? Bob's in a wheelchair, paralyzed on the right side, with some tubes still in him, wearing a bicycle helmet to protect his "missing" left bone flap, and we're eating our dinner in a dreary dining hall in a run-down nursing home.

Wasn't the best birthday ever the one when the four of us were at the beach and threw him the Three Stooges party and had a whipped-cream-pie fight in the backyard? Or the one when the kids decorated the dining room like a baseball field and used real bases as place mats? Or the one at Donna and Jim's, where we had the big family party at the lake, and he got his Goody Two Shoes plaque from his cousins, who never remembered him getting into trouble as a kid? Those all *sound* a helluva lot better. But today Bob's brother is celebrating with him in person for the first time in probably fifty years, Bob is teasing Ben the Younger about the food on his chin, and Ben is giving it right back at him: "I'll wipe mine if you wipe yours!" When Bob comments on his birthday by saying he's made it another year, the three of us can't help blurting out, "Just barely!" This is the birthday that almost wasn't, but it is. And it is the best.

Friday, July 25, 2014

The hits keep coming. Today I was walking into the building when I was stopped by the speech therapist who wanted to let me know that Bob had some news for me. She couldn't resist and told me that Mary, the physical therapist, had been in bed with Bob. *Hmm.* Perhaps Mr. Bucceri has some 'splaining to do. So, enjoying the prank, I go upstairs to Bob's room and ask him, "What's this I hear about you being in bed with Mary?"

He gives me a surprised look and says in all seriousness, "Wait, it wasn't what you think. It wasn't like that." And then he tells me, and it is clear that the news is for real, and it is big. In therapy today he stayed in his room instead of going to the rehab room. Mary had him lie on his bed on his left hip, and then she worked with Bob to concentrate on lifting and lowering his right leg in a controlled manner. It took a lot of effort, but he did it, several times.

This is huge news, because until now Bob has not been able to move his right leg by himself at all. In fact, he was beginning to think it was dead. True, he had been in walking therapy and had succeeded in going over forty feet in one stretch. But it had required therapists to manipulate the right leg, and it was not yet evident whether he would be able to power the right leg on his own. Today it became clear that his brain is reconnecting and firing the muscles in his right leg. Another seminal moment in this journey, another reason to celebrate, and another reason to make sure he gets to the acute rehab as soon as possible—insurance company be damned!

Job one on Monday morning will be to finalize his admission and transfer to acute inpatient rehab, so he can continue his trajectory. In the meantime, this weekend we will work on standing, muscle tone, chair transfers, and concentration games. Semper avanti.

Saturday, July 26, 2014

"There's something about Mary." In therapy this afternoon Bob does two series of walking, traveling about ten feet in each series. True, that is about one-fourth the distance of his personal best of just a few days ago. But here is the difference: today the steps he makes with his right leg are made under his own power. He lifts the right leg and moves the foot forward about twelve inches. The therapist simply guides the landing of the foot to make sure it is straight. I will take ten feet under those conditions any day, and the therapists agree.

At the end of his session, Bob typically hooks his left leg under the right and lifts both with the left so the therapist can wheel him back to where they started. That act that would be simple for us is a process for him. But today, as he sits, and the therapists are busy talking to each other, I notice him lifting the right leg and uncrossing it from the left. "Hey, did anyone see that?" I yell.

"What? What?" asks Bob. The therapists burst out laughing and say yes, they caught that. Not only does Bob uncross his right leg, he apparently does it "without thinking"!

Watching the therapy sessions and realizing what Bob is dealing with has been a fascinating and frustrating lesson in the workings of the brain. Some actions are fully back in play, like taking a spoonful of food and placing it in his mouth, chewing it, and swallowing it. But if the spoon is empty, or the handle is on the right side of the bowl, he has to make the mental connection of how to get the spoon over to the other side, load it up, and take it from there.

This morning he wants to cut the pieces of his frittata in half using the side of his fork. Concentrate as he might, that connection cannot be made, and so I help. The therapist refers to it as motor planning, and it consists largely of movements we take for granted. Likewise with the exercises. Today we do abs. It takes many minutes for him to make the connection between his brain and his torso to do a controlled sit-up and come back down. But once he makes the connection, he can do the three sets in steady progression. I admire how he does not get frustrated. He knows what he has to reconnect, and he seems patient to keep working at it until it comes. I think the fact that he has seen such advances over the past week and a half helps him be patient, because he knows he is making progress. The idea that his right leg is "starting to fire again," as he says it, has been a huge source of motivation for him.

As for me, during a girl's morning out today, new nails and new hair will hopefully put to rest any questions from strangers about Bob being my son or me being a cougar. Semper avanti.

Tuesday, July 29, 2014

I throw out a Hail Mary and have Bob transferred to acute rehab in the late morning under private pay. By two thirty in the afternoon, we receive word that the external reviewer overturned the insurance company's denial. He's in! They have pre-certified seven days. "We'll take it!" I cry. When the seven days are up, we will have to go for another pre-certification. And there remains a question about the last fourteen days at the nursing home and whether or not insurance will pick that up, so that is for follow-up tomorrow. But it doesn't matter anymore. He is in the best place he can possibly be, and for that we are grateful. Compared to the dingy décor of the nursing home, the acute rehab is the Ritz Carlton. It is bright and cheerful and smells clean. There is a garden, a gazebo, and a fish pond. But the real and most important difference is that he will be kept safe from falls and under the direction and daily care of a behavioral neurologist; a physiatrist; and a team of nurses and physical, occupational, and speech therapists who specialize in brain-injury recovery.

The relief we both feel is indescribable. I know he is nervous about it—a little scared, even. He has a long road to travel yet, but he has come so far, and he will do great things. He will start therapy tomorrow, and they do not mess around. No loosey-goosey visiting hours like at the nursing home. Visitors are welcome between 4:00 p.m. and 9:00 p.m. daily. Prior to 4:00 p.m. he could be in therapy at any given time, and visitors are not recommended because of the distraction. No one is allowed to attend sessions except caregivers receiving training. I am not even sure I can play the wife card.

So visitors are still very welcome and very much needed but mostly during weekday late afternoons and evenings and on weekends. Bob told me about a week ago he didn't think he could do this without the support of all the visitors he has been getting. We are forever grateful to everyone out there who has been able to give him their time. We are so appreciative. He is now in the brain-injury unit, where he belongs.

I still may not sleep like a baby, but I will certainly start to sleep better than I have been—at least for the next seven days. Semper avanti.

NaN*Nancy Bucceri*

NaN**Thursday, July 31, 2014**

NaN**Well, it took rehab a** couple of days of assessment and orientation
to get down to it in full force, but today they did just that. They
worked Bob's right arm for a full thirty minutes. He said it was
painful, but he knew it needed to be done, and he was glad for the
workout. I told him that this is what makes him a model patient:
he is not afraid to work through pain to get to his end goal. He
agreed: no pain, no gain. Or to put my philosophical spin on it,
it was Socrates who said where there is no pain, there can be no
pleasure.

NaNBob did thirty minutes of walking, speech therapy at lunch,
and occupational therapy in the morning and afternoon. All good.
He worked with the speech therapist to change his diet to regular
soft food instead of chopped soft food, and he actually ate a green
salad for dinner.

NaNHe had a psychological evaluation today too, which is something
he did not have at the nursing home. He told the therapist that
rather than focus on what had happened to him he wanted to
focus on moving forward. He's got that *semper avanti* rap down
cold, I thought to myself. He stated his most immediate goal: get
well enough to go home. He has other goals: Clearwater, Florida for
the Electronic Benefits Transfer (EBT) conference in early November;
Thanksgiving with family at our house in late November; and Julia's
college graduation in May. At one time I looked at the Clearwater
trip as an impossibility, with the best case being a real stretch goal,
but I am not so sure anymore. It all seems doable.

NaNOne of the challenges he is facing is his sense of time. The
therapy room is right around the corner from his room, so there
is not a lot of travel time to places, and there is a lot of dead time
between therapies. He can either be in his wheelchair or in his bed
when he is not in therapy, and so he says that it is easy to get caught
in a day and not really know whether it is lunchtime or dinnertime
or even what day of the week it is. We bring him the newspapers,

and he has his iPad and phone to connect him to the outside world. He and I have called each other a few times, and it feels great to be able to reach out and connect like that again. But it is still easy for him to lose track of time.

This evening we enjoyed our visit out by the koi pond, and we actually saw a few snapping turtles. When our friend Fritz told Bob how impressed he was with his attitude and determination, Bob told him point-blank it was because of visits from friends like him and our family. He said that friends and family remind him of the good life that awaits him. There is life happening outside the rehab hospital, and he wants to be reminded of it every day so he can continue to motivate himself to get better.

Tomorrow Ben the Elder will leave and return to his life and family in Sacramento. It has been a wonderful time, having him here with us. I know he came to help Bob, and help him he did, but it helped our whole family, too.

Tonight our Ceci will be arriving for a week, and I know Bob can't wait to spend time with her. We call Julia "Ceci" because that is what we thought she looked like when we first saw her on the ultrasound of my womb—a little *ceci* bean. Then our niece and her family will arrive on their way to the beach house we rented together. I will have a full house for a day or so before I head down to the beach with them to get them settled into the house and show them the lay of the land. I won't be staying long; in fact, I will be back late Monday, but in the meantime Bob will have Julia and Ben giving him lots of love and attention and then they will head to the beach for a quick stay. None of us feels up to a week at the beach with Bob in the hospital, and our niece understands.

I know the summer will move more quickly now. Ben will be heading back to Temple in a few weeks. I can't think of that now. I'll think about that tomorrow. For tonight, I will think about all we are blessed with. Semper avanti.

Sunday, August 3, 2014

It is a rainy, gray, and lazy day at the beach. I am here with our niece and her family, getting them acclimated to our favorite beach town, Bethany Beach, Delaware. So while I am sitting here with the sound of the breaking waves coming through our porch door, Bob is at the rehab hospital, continuing to make astounding progress. This morning's session involved, among other things, using his left leg to step up onto a box and lift his body up to a standing position on the box. He said it is extremely hard, but he did it. It requires him to bear all his weight on the right leg, the leg that a week ago he had just started to move ever so slightly. This follows the work he reported to us on Friday, when he walked the length of his unit corridor three times with minimal assistance and stood for fifteen minutes.

In occupational therapy he is getting a lot of work on his right arm, and he says that has been painful. But he knows it is necessary to get the arm "firing" again, as he puts it, so he works through it. Yesterday his complaint to me was that he had wasted a day: no therapy. I reminded him how he'd always taught me to take a day off between weight-lifting days, and that this was like that. It was not a wasted day but a day of rest, and he will be working the next six days. His job on his non-therapy day, I told him, is to work at resting. He is impatient, I know. He is approaching his third month of hospitalization, so I can only imagine how tired of that he is.

Before talking to Bob, I was able to talk to my nephew, who is also in a hospital, a sterile room protecting him as the doctors treat him for complications from his bone marrow transplant. I will try to connect Etienne and Bob; they might Skype each other and trade stories about their respective "incarcerations." From what I understand, there is finally a place in France where the food is bad.

Bob cherishes his visitors, and it is hard to be at the beach without him, but we promised each other another beach vacation to make up for it. I will be heading back home tomorrow. Bob has an

MRI follow-up scheduled at the medical center, so we are interested to hear the results of that. He wants his skull back, he says, so he doesn't have to feel like Cro-Magnon man anymore. I tell him he's going to have to at least trim that beard if he really wants to do that! Semper avanti.

Wednesday, August 6, 2014

I write this just after the kids and I are back from one final visit with "the crew" together before Julia heads back to Pittsburgh for the remainder of the summer and the beginning of her senior year. We have a birthday celebration of sorts, so we can give Bob his present together. We have ice cream, brownies, and almost two hours outside just shooting the breeze as we often would do on a summer evening when we'd eat outside on the deck.

Bob loves his gift and actually puts it on. It's an official 2014 All-Star Game batting jersey: Number 2, Derek Jeter, of course. It was a lovely, intimate family party.

Bob and I met with the case manager yesterday and learned that the insurance company has approved another week. She assures us that it will not be a problem for us now that Bob is actually there. I still have the issue of the last two weeks at the nursing home, which the insurance company has already told us they will deny. I will fight that, but my sense of urgency is gone now that Bob is where he needs to be and progressing so well.

After Bob's first week of therapy, the care team has assessed very good progress and very promising goals, with an estimated four to six weeks remaining at the acute rehab before Bob can transition to outpatient. The goals can change on a weekly basis, so nothing is set in stone, but that is their estimate for now.

We don't have word on the MRI of the brain yet, and there's no ETA on the cranioplasty. Is that what it's called? I keep calling it a reverse craniotomy, but the bottom line is we don't yet know when the surgery to replace his skull will be. Anyway, with that simple surgery will come even more improvement in cognitive healing, so we anxiously await that.

Today they put Bob on a treadmill machine with a harness, called a Lokomat, while he was taken through thirty minutes of steady walking movement to retrain the brain. Intense therapy on his right arm has made it a little more flexible so it can be positioned on a special armrest on the wheelchair, but an x-ray reveals there may be some injury that needs to be addressed before therapy can continue. An MRI is scheduled for tomorrow. Too bad that wasn't identified before the MRI that was done on Monday!

Cognitive and speech therapy are progressing well, and psychological therapy is being used to help stave off depression and other emotional issues that can arise as a result of such a devastating injury and rehabilitation. Never one to be patient, Bob is longing to come home and is worried about his arm. It bothered me to hear him tell a nurse, "What do I have to smile about?" when she said she'd love to see him smile more.

So I told him. "You've got us! Your crew!"

And he replied, "Yes, you are right, and I have this swanky jersey!" So, unusually deadpan delivery aside, we do see the sense of humor coming through once in a while.

I broke the news that I may need to go to Dallas for a few days the last week of August, and that will leave him without coverage, as he puts it. The kids will both be back at school by then. Thank God he has his phone and we can call him every day. He does not have the dexterity to text yet, but he has his lifeline to the outside world through phone calls.

So progress continues, and we are healing. Semper avanti.

Sunday, August 10, 2014

Except for the fact that we are sitting in a lounge area of the rehab hospital, Bob and I are spending a rather typical Sunday reading the paper and drinking coffee. I made our weekly trek to Wegman's by myself this morning. The coffee bar ladies always ask how Bob is doing, so in some ways it is as if he is with me anyway.

Bob's progress is very good. It is hard for me to see it because I am not present when all this therapy is going on, so I rely on what he is telling me, and what he is telling me sounds very promising indeed. Occupational therapists have been working with him on his right arm, but right now that is a little on hold because the MRI indicated two sprained ligaments. So as a way to keep making some progress, the therapist has started working his hand.

Yesterday, for the very first time since May, Bob was able to squeeze the therapist's fingers with his right hand! This is huge—especially since his regular therapist told him just the other day that he probably would not regain full use of it. I am no expert, but it seems to me that if the brain connection can be made once in therapy and then again the next day, as Bob reported this morning, it is a connection that can be made over and over until it is back.

Visitors continue to arrive from all over: boyhood friends, business colleagues, neighbors, family. These visits are the highlight of Bob's week, and it moves us both very much. My niece Marianne, her husband, Renan, and their children have returned from the beach and will be heading back to France tomorrow. It has been great seeing them, even if it wasn't the way we had planned it. Semper avanti.

Tuesday, August 12, 2014

Today marks the three-month anniversary of Bob's stroke. I feel as though I have lived a lifetime since May. Bob continues his progress. In rehab terms, he is moving from maximum assist to moderate assist in some things and requiring only minimal assist in others. It is estimated he will be there through September 10. His cognitive skills are strong and coming back well. His biggest problem seems to be the pain in his right arm and the fact that therapy can't continue until he sees an orthopedic doctor. That will happen this week.

I realized this weekend that sometimes I am too close to the situation to see progress. Our two grandnephews, ages seven and eleven, noticed right away on Sunday that Uncle Bob had more facial expression than just the week before. They noticed him smiling and laughing a little more. It made me happy just to know they'd noticed that. I had missed it.

Tonight is an extra special night out for me, as I am treated to dinner with neighborhood friends. We visit Bob together ahead of our reservation time, and Ben stops by to see his dad before heading to the beach for a day with friends. It is a nice evening, despite the rain, as we laugh about old times and new. I have known some of these women for as long as twenty-one years. The Clover Ridge Cougars. That's what I will call us from now on.

Sunday, August 17, 2014

Last week was a big week for us, and this week coming up promises to be bigger still. Although Bob is experiencing periodic pain in his right arm throughout the day, the MRI revealed nothing requiring surgery. That is good news, and with it comes a new therapy plan expected this week. On Friday I took a half-day off work to observe therapy and meet the team. I witnessed the Lokomat, which is a robotic treadmill that helps the patient take about a thousand steps at a session with the purpose of retraining the brain to tell the legs how to walk. A patient must be able to stand for twenty minutes and must be able to do some of the work. In the four times that Bob has done it, he has begun to stand straighter, and the therapists say he is increasing his workload, though they do not tell me by how much. After the Lokomat, they typically do ten to fifteen minutes of floor walking. Bob still requires two therapists to assist because he does not have much strength in or control over the right leg, but progress is being made. In fact, on Saturday his weekend therapist got him to bend his right knee while lying on a mat and to do most of the work to roll onto his side so he could get into a seated position. She also had him do many repetitions of stepping his left leg onto a box and then back down, necessitating him to bear all his weight on his right leg. Earlier in the day he'd felt he had been on a plateau the past several days, but by Saturday afternoon he had some new, significant progress to give him the boost he needed to keep his spirits up.

Both the psychologist and speech therapist tell me that Bob's language skills are nothing short of astounding. They both say he must not be wired the same as most people. I could have told them that. Anyway, with that said, he requires breathing therapy to bring power to his voice, and cognitive therapy to hone what they call executive-level thinking. Similar to retraining the brain to tell the legs they can walk, he needs repetitive exercises to help him relearn attention to detail, multitasking, and other problem-solving skills.

This is where it gets interesting: On Friday the therapist reported that Bob could identify only about half the words in front of him that contained the letters *N* and *T.* But on Sunday afternoon, when I suddenly lose my train of thought during a conversation, it's Bob who tells me what I was talking about and gets me back on track. That was not lost on our visiting friends and son, who couldn't help but tease me about it. And Bob's response to that used his typical brand of humor: he reassured us all that we were in the right place if any of us needed help with brain function!

This coming week will include a visit to the neurosurgeon at the academic medical center to find out the results of the MRI. We are very eager to hear when the doctor thinks the cranioplasty can be done. As Bob asked me the other day, "Any idea when they will put Humpty Dumpty back together again?" Hopefully we will find out soon.

The week was also marked by Julia's twenty-second birthday— our Marian baby, born on the Feast of the Assumption of Mary on August 15, 1992. Julia Elizabeth was named for my great-aunt Julia, who lived with my family until she was almost 102, and my mother, Elizabeth, who everyone called Betty. While most babies are considered gifts by their parents, Julia literally was a GIFT. It stands for gamete intrafallopian transfer; she was born after six years of infertility treatments.

Although Julia was far away in Pittsburgh, we tried to help her celebrate by phone. I enjoyed my own moment reflecting on the memory of her birth, how it felt like a lifetime ago and yet just yesterday all at the same time. How could that be? I reflected back on Bob spending Saturdays with her while I pursued my master's degree, the two of them taking trips to the farmers' market and spending "full Sundays in the workshop" making treasures together out of wood scraps. I recalled when, at the age of two, and upon learning her father would be taking her to the Philadelphia Auto Show, she'd politely traded in the overalls and turtleneck I had selected for a dress, tights, and her best Mary Janes. The auto show is still a favorite of theirs; it eventually replaced the annual father-daughter dance that had marked every winter since Julia was in first grade. Julia reminds me so much of her dad: bright, gorgeous, funny, and possessing that uncanny ability to remember everything she learns.

Tuesday, August 19, 2014

So today is interesting. The diagnosis of the right-arm pain is that the chest muscles are so tight that they are pulling on the shoulder muscles, which in turn are pulling on the upper-back muscles. This is what is causing so much pain and making it very difficult to make much progress. So the therapy is a shot of Botox to the chest. This nerve block will cause the chest muscle to weaken over the next two to three weeks, allowing for better manipulation of the arm and related muscles during therapy. The effect of the Botox will last about three months, by which time the expectation is that the muscles might be able to stay looser on their own. Bob explains all this to Ben, who says, "So, basically, you got a boob job."

In speech therapy Bob has been learning some techniques to encourage speaking on exhalation, so he can start to get some more power to his voice.

All in all, he reported a good day today, boob job notwithstanding.

Wednesday, August 20, 2014

I know this journal has been about Bob and his illness and recovery. But it has also been about our family, and tonight there is another member of our family who needs the monster prayer chain that has been helping Bob these past three months. I have been so moved by the more than twelve thousand visits to my blog. So I am praying tonight that everyone who has been reading about Bob will see this and extend prayers to our nephew Etienne. Etienne is in a medically induced coma, fighting for his life after having gone through what we all had hoped would be a successful bone marrow transplant a few months back. But he developed a serious infection last Friday, after he had been released from the hospital following other complications. He, his lovely partner, Emma, and four-year-old son, Nathan, need our prayers. Lots of them.

Friday, August 22, 2014

Tonight is date night, just like the ones we had a lifetime ago, when we'd put the babies to bed and have a romantic takeout dinner by the fireplace and just spend the night talking or maybe watching a movie. Bob had called me earlier in the day with the idea, and he tells the nurse as we wheel past, "We're going out for dinner. Be back in an hour." And so we go twenty feet out the back door and sit at a table near the trees and grass, with our Wawa hoagie dinner and sodas. Delicious! After we talk for a while, we go back upstairs and watch *Wait Until Dark* with Audrey Hepburn. Alan Arkin still makes my skin crawl when I watch that movie. We talk some more about everything: the kids, road trips we want to take, how scary that movie was, dreams that are so real they are sometimes hard to separate from reality … It is a really nice date night.

Date night aside, I receive an update on Bob's situation after his visit to the neurosurgeon on Wednesday. Except for the five-hour delay getting him back to rehab after the appointment in the city (don't ask!) it went well. The bottom line is that all systems are go for the cranioplasty—except, of course, for the minor detail that we don't actually have the cranio needed to do the plasty. It is still in a freezer somewhere in Virginia.

Not to digress, but this actually reminds me of my mother and a story she would often tell about her cooking mishaps. One night while preparing dinner, she mixed two seemingly identical containers from the freezer and accidentally served caramel-giblet sauce over ice cream. The best part of the story to me was always how everyone was so polite as they tried to figure out what those horrible soft nuts were and then how to spit the stuff out without hurting her feelings. Anyway, back to Bob's cranioplasty. I'll assume Virginia has better freezer labels than my mother did back in 1960!

I whipped out the phone number and contact name for the bone flap and gave it to the neurosurgeon's office staff. We are hoping to get it shipped up here and the procedure done in a few weeks. I'll spare you all the long conversation over whether or not they'd be able to accept the bone from Virginia, because it might not be a certified bone bank, or it might not meet Pennsylvania's standards or those of the academic medical center, or whatever. These organizations can be so full of themselves! We're not talking *West* Virginia, for goodness' sake. Anyway, before the cranioplasty, the surgeon wants to do another angiogram to try to figure out what caused the bleed in the first place. Unfortunately, neither the recent MRI nor the CAT scan revealed anything about that. The surgeon also wants to do a few other tests related to vision and hormone balance because of a moderate-sized tumor that was found behind the pituitary gland. There are no apparent effects from the tumor, but of course we'll need to be watching that from now on.

Bob continues to make slow but steady progress. His right arm is still painful, but he did enough therapy today that he was able to achieve a little more movement in a couple of fingers. The surgeon was a little pessimistic about his hand, but I say if you can move a finger once, you can move it a thousand times. Semper avanti.

Tuesday, August 26, 2014

Over the weekend Bob's occupational therapist was able to stimulate his triceps muscle on the right side, and he was able to move some fingers again. The pain is still bad, but it has not even been a week since the Botox injection, so patience is needed. It's still a good sign—the movement, that is.

We are now separated by fourteen hundred miles while I am in Dallas for meetings. It feels a little unsettling to be so far away, but Bob and I are able to connect by phone, so that is good. His cousins Ernie and Judy are at the house, so he's getting some more of that boot-camp therapy during visits from yet another former marine in the family.

Bob tells me over the phone that he has a full schedule of therapy, including trying out different leg braces that help him walk unassisted. The one that helps him the most he doesn't like, because it goes from his toes to his thigh. It is too big and heavy, he says. His view is that he isn't doing the walking, the brace is doing the walking. But I suggest that he accept it as a temporary measure. Only time will tell what, if anything, he will need over the long haul. Semper avanti.

Friday, August 29, 2014

My meetings in Dallas this week were all successful, and it was great to be fully engaged in person with my colleagues and leadership team. I conducted three presentations, one involving a business case I had prepared for the executives that was quite well received. But it also feels great to be heading home.

While I was gone, Bob continued his hard work in his determination toward recovery. His stay at the rehab facility will extend until September 24, due to continued progress. The specific date for the cranioplasty is still to be determined, but it will likely be scheduled prior to the twenty-fourth. The angiogram that we hope reveal the cause of the bleed is scheduled for September 11.

Progress continues. His walking is improving steadily though slowly. A new electronic stimulation therapy will be used in an effort to stimulate his quadriceps. He still requires two therapists to assist with walking, but he has improved to needing only minimal assist on the left with moderate on the right. He is doing wheelchair transfers with minimal assistance and continues to improve his balance when standing.

Bob's motor-planning skills are still a challenge; he requires guidance to put one foot in front of the other and other similar instructions from the therapist. His long-term memory is fully intact, and he retains a lot of new information, especially about news, his treatment, and therapies. I don't understand the difference between remembering to lift and move a foot and remembering an article in the newspaper, but it clearly is a different set of brain functions.

His speech continues to progress, due largely to his own initiative to work on his breathing with a spirometer as well as his regular speech-therapy sessions.

My next business trip is set for late September; it will be a management retreat. I am arranging agency assistance in the event that Bob is home then.

As I reflect back on the summer, at the start of this Labor Day weekend, I continue to be grateful for the recovery that Bob is experiencing. On Memorial Day weekend Bob was just beginning to stir from his coma, and it was almost another two weeks before he fully woke up. His ability to function at that time was still unknown.

Now he is fully alert and articulate. He is fully engaged with his therapists and slowly reclaiming his life. Semper avanti.

Saturday, August 30, 2014

I spent the better part of today with Bob and watched him walk a hundred feet with no assistance on the left and moderate assistance on the right. He has come so far in just three and a half months; he is an inspiration to me. But my heart is very heavy tonight with the loss of our nephew Etienne. His hard-fought battle is over, his journey ended. It is a tragedy that I am having a hard time wrapping my head around. I think back on the Sunday morning in January when I opened my email to a surprise photo of Julia with Marianne, Etienne, and their families all having brunch together at Marianne's home near Paris, France. That day was doubly joyful as we learned a marrow donor for Etienne had been found. I am grateful for the two days I was able to spend with Etienne, his partner, and little boy in March when I visited my sister and her husband in France. I am grateful for the conversations he and I had in recent weeks and the way we made each other laugh. With his passing, I am reminded once again how fragile life is, how painful it can be, and how it must be cherished. Life is a gift, and I am grateful for the gift that was Etienne.

Friday, September 5, 2014

This was a quiet week of work, visiting Bob, and continuing his advocacy. Etienne was laid to rest today, so my heart and thoughts were an ocean away with my sister's family, Etienne's partner, Emma, and their little boy, Nathan, in Nantes, France.

Bob is progressing well but growing more and more homesick as the time goes on. Who can blame him? He has been "incarcerated" now for almost four months; it has been a long and arduous journey. Progress continues, although the pain in his right arm continues as well. I keep reminding myself that the Botox will not be fully in play until early next week, so we need to be patient a little longer.

As Bob's advocate, I have been preparing the necessary documentation for phase two of our fight with the insurance company. As they said they would, they denied the claim for the last two weeks' stay and therapies at the nursing home in July. I have also had to continue to serve as chief organizer of all things associated with health care. Bob had a CAT scan scheduled for Thursday at the medical center. But why? No one could tell me, and the nurse practitioner from the surgeon's office did not return my calls. Why a CAT scan? Why the medical center? I am glad I intervened because when I finally got through to people, we learned it was not needed after all; it turned out to be a leftover order from the previous month.

Thankfully Bob was spared a miserable ride to the city and a lost day of therapy. Then my attention turned to the cranioplasty and why the wheels were not yet in motion to get the bone flap sent up here and the surgery scheduled. I really, really don't want him discharged home with his head still exposed like that. I made several phone calls yesterday and today but have no real answers yet.

In the meantime, I will share Bob's latest experience in speech therapy. When he first got his voice back, in July, it quickly gained both volume and clarity, but in recent weeks it seems to have weakened a bit. So Bob went to his therapist about it, and together they devised a plan for getting him back on track. She decided to capitalize on his sports coaching, recognizing that one needs to yell from the dugout to be heard. Her plan was to have Bob record several common phrases he says to his players, as if he were in the dugout and the players were in the field, and then she would play them back for Bob to hear and see where he needed to improve. So Bob came up with three standbys to start with: "Get a good pitch to hit!"; "Make him throw you a good pitch!"; and "Wait for your pitch!" He spoke them loudly, and he and Jessica seemed pleased, so they decided to play back the recording. What they heard sent them both rolling with laughter: "Get a good bitch to hit!"; "Wait for your bitch!"; and Jessica's favorite, "Make him throw you a good bitch!" Back to speech therapy. Semper avanti.

Thursday, September 11, 2014

◇◇◇◇

Once again we have been stymied by the dysfunction of our health care system. Bob was supposed to get his angiogram today, a prerequisite to the cranioplasty, which still has not been scheduled, despite his pending discharge in two weeks. But he didn't have an angiogram; he had a CAT scan. But he didn't need a CAT scan, he needed an angiogram. And the neurosurgeon's office confirmed for me last night that he did not need the CAT scan and that it had been cancelled. No one could tell me who had reordered the CAT scan or why—and they could not tell me who cancelled the angiogram or why, and they could not reschedule the angiogram, because that needed a doctor's order. Hard as I worked last week to save Bob a CAT scan and get him scheduled for the angiogram and cranioplasty, I might as well have been talking into a Fisher-Price telephone.

We are no further along now than we were last week. I fear how this is all going to end: the rehab and medical center will not be able to get this thing coordinated. Bob will be discharged to home without his skull back in one piece, putting the last four months of recovery at great risk. It is beyond absurd, but I can't control it. Rational thought and logic mean nothing. There is no such thing as "staying on top" of things in health care. Just yesterday I had confirmed everything, or so I thought, with the rehab case manager and the neurosurgeon's nurse practitioner, the two coordinators on each end. It made absolutely no difference.

Sunday, September 14, 2014

◇◇◇◇

Here we sit by the koi pond, Bob dozing in the warm sun after our fall picnic lunch. It is a gorgeous, cool autumn day and this weekend marks four months since his stroke. We are both growing weary of this phase and anxious to start the next one. But at the same time, I am anxious about what our new normal at home will be. To help prepare, I will be attending another half day of therapy on Tuesday. I need some idea of what modifications will be needed in the house besides strategically placed grab bars in the bathrooms and elsewhere. I have estimates and lead times for some things but have held off doing anything until I have a better sense of what will be needed temporarily and what will be needed permanently.

Anticipating another mandatory business trip to Dallas the week of October 6, I am working on securing a private duty nurse to stay with Bob and help him out for those five days. There are lots of changes, but all are still taking us forward. We have promised each other that once we spring him from this joint we will spend every weekend doing something fun, big or small. Semper avanti.

Tuesday, September 16, 2014

"We reach our future one day at a time." Those are the words of wisdom Bob imparts on us today as we meet with the psychologist at the end of my half-day of observing Bob's therapies. It is an emotional but productive meeting, and while I forget whom Bob was quoting, the words resonate with me. This whole experience has required patience that neither Bob nor I ever possessed before. It requires us to accept the fact that we can set goals but we can't attach timelines to those goals. That is not my way. This is so hard. When it comes to a brain injury, there is no such thing as a deadline. It requires us to stay focused and determined. At least I can do that.

This is where we are now: Wheelchair transfers are pretty easy, with Bob doing 90–100 percent of the work. Walking is progressing, though it still requires therapist assistance, mostly because of the motor planning and sense of balance that goes with it. The brace helps, but it does not yet give him independence. A home assessment will be conducted on Thursday morning, so I will get a better sense of home modifications that will be required. Our narrow doorway openings are a major concern, given the assumption that Bob will still be heavily dependent on the wheelchair for getting from point A to point B. My earlier estimates for things like a stair lift and wheelchair ramps will serve me well if I need to get work scheduled in the next week or so. I know the lead times and who to call.

We meet with a private-duty nursing agency that comes highly recommended. This is for my upcoming five-day trip to Dallas. While my first conversation with an agency ended with them asking me whether I had a backup, in case their caregiver called out, this agency is guaranteeing me coverage. By the way, why would I be calling a private-duty nursing agency to back me up if I already had a backup?

As Bob and I both tell the psychologist, we are so very tired of this and just want to go home. But going home brings unknowns, and that is scary. What makes it hopeful is that progress continues. We are not at the end of the possibilities. Hell, Bob doesn't even have his skull back yet! Our goal of going to Clearwater for the EBT conference is not unrealistic, while at one time it seemed unquestionably out of reach.

So, all in all, it has been a good day. We have observed a lot, shared a lot, and shed and dried tears. Semper avanti.

Thursday, September 18, 2014
◇◇◇◇

The therapists visit our home today and provide the much-needed assessment on the house. My overarching goal is to find a way to make sure Bob can come back to our home and live in it much as before without doing any real structural changes if we can avoid it. All the research I have been doing about handicap accessibility in homes has been making me very nervous. A major hurdle is solved immediately when I am shown how to get him into the house without using any wheelchair ramp. I get the OT,

Mike—all 225 pounds of him—into the house through the front door. *Hoo-yah!* Next is the interior. We toss about some ideas: Bed in the office? (No, he needs his office to be an office.) Bed in the living room or family room? (Hmm, not liking it. He wants to sleep in his own bed.) Sponge bathe in the laundry-room utility sink? (Maybe for one day.) Portable shower in the foyer or living room? (What? Hell no!) Stair climber device? (I'm listening.) Transport chair upstairs for moving through narrow doorways? (I like it, I like it.) Replace master bath glass shower door with curtain, portable bench, handheld shower head, and grab bars? (great idea). Sleep in Julia's bed? (Now you're losing me again.) Take master bed off four-poster so it sits lower to the floor? (Okay, getting warmer.) Switch sides of the bed? (Seriously? After thirty-two years?)

So that is the bulk of it. I will try a portable ramp for the deck, just to make it a little easier. The first-floor powder room will be a challenge until Bob is a little steadier on his feet, but offset hinges may help, and as Bob said when I reported back all the ideas, "Maybe I'll just go upstairs." Ha! We didn't even think of that, and we are not the ones with brain injury.

Sunday, September 21, 2014

We are in the run-up to discharge, and although this next phase promises more testing of our mettle and challenges that we may not full appreciate, we are raring to go. Yesterday during occupational therapy I witnessed something so fascinating it took my breath away. The therapist used an over-the-counter electronic massage device called Magic Wand. Magic indeed. His baseline was to tell Bob to kick up his right foot, and Bob was able to concentrate enough to move the right foot about an inch off the ground. The therapist then placed the wand on Bob's right thigh and told him to kick up with his right foot. Bob was able to easily comply, getting the foot about eight inches off the ground. Removing the wand so Bob was "flying solo," he then told Bob to hold his position, and then after a few seconds told him to slowly lower his foot to the ground. Bob was able to comply with both commands. To my non-medical, uneducated eye, it was … magic! The therapist explained that this indicated two things: first that the leg muscles are responsive, and second that the brain is able to communicate to the leg and foot. The therapist agreed that this was "a good sign," and "very encouraging." Me? I'm losing my freaking mind. This is nothing short of amazing and convinces me that there will come a day when Bob will walk again.

This morning Bob called me while I was dutifully out shopping for grab bars, handheld showerheads, and other fun durable medical equipment, to tell me I'd missed the best part. He'd had a sixty-minute therapy session with the Magic Wand again. This time the therapist had been able to get Bob's right arm to straighten itself out, open and close the five fingers, and make a fist to the point where the fingers curled into the palm of his hand. This was a first. In another exercise, he'd been able to bend to his toes and touch them. I couldn't believe I'd missed it.

In the meantime, we are waiting for confirmation of when the angiogram (we think it is this week), the cranioplasty and the discharge will be. It is quite possible that Bob will be discharged on October 1, with the cranioplasty to follow the week of October 6. If that happens, I will need to go to plan B, because I am expected in Dallas during that time. I am not sure what plan B will be, but if the surgery is that week, it will entail my being here. As much as Bob wants this surgery, he is beginning to get a little anxious about it, so he will need moral support going into it.

We continue to be blessed (and spoiled) by the company of good friends. Bob receives regular visits by local business colleagues and friends, and we were treated to picnic dinners twice this week, at which we just sat around the table and enjoyed good food, laughter and storytelling, and just talking about our crazy jobs and kids. These are some of life's simple pleasures, and we have been enjoying them. Semper avanti.

Friday, September 26, 2014

"Nothing going on upstairs" is not a phrase anyone would ever use to describe Bob. But that is exactly what the results of the angiogram show: no indications of any lesions, aneurisms, oversized veins, or anything. There are no abnormalities. So while it does not explain the cause of the original bleed, it does indicate that all systems are go for the cranioplasty. That is great news!

I spend another half-day in therapy, and it is productive, although Bob's activities are curtailed a bit because of the angiogram. That procedure starts at the femoral artery in the groin, so no strenuous walking is allowed for today. We do practice car transfers, putting on the brace and standing up, locking it, etc. And in occupational therapy I learn how to do range-of-motion exercises and stretches on the right arm and hand. I observe speech therapy, which is focused more on multitasking, motor planning, and quick thinking, and we have another good session with the psychologist. We are both getting a little emotional as we approach phase four. Bob is understandably anxious about hurting his head again once he gets out of there, but as the therapist reminded us both, once his skull is back his head will be no more at risk than anyone else's. We want the next phase to start, but a little relieved that it will wait until the skull is back in, the feeding tube is out, and he'll be a little stronger. Semper avanti.

Friday, October 3, 2014

Bob started the week on double-secret probation for deciding to get out of bed unassisted on Sunday. Luckily no harm was done, except possibly to the nurse who had just left the room after Bob had asked for help in getting dressed. The doctor seemed to understand Bob's point of view and actually apologized that the nurse had not taken more time to explain to him why she'd had to leave.

We are now preparing for Bob's discharge after the upcoming surgery October 9. With the kind help of friends and relatives, the house has been modified to accommodate Bob's needs. Grab bars are on, the glass shower doors have been replaced with a curtain, and we are ready with an access ramp into the house. Our mattress and box spring have been taken off the frame and now sit on the floor. Throw in a Beatles poster and lava lamp and the room will look like a throw-back to the sixties. The stair glide is in and working well. There are a few odds and ends left to do, but I feel I can at least get him home and get us started.

We are both so ready to be back together again, so ready to have Bob home where he belongs. But I don't know what I don't know, and I am feeling some anxiety over it. Today I learn how to assist Bob with a shower and dressing. That goes well. Then I learn how to bump his wheelchair down and out of the house—or off a sidewalk or single step—backward. It's what you do when there is no ramp. I only make his teeth chatter once, so I'm thinking that I did pretty well. I then assist on the left as he walks about two hundred feet. While walking is still reserved for therapy, I can feel he is stronger and his steps are smoother; there's more of a flow than a stop and start now. It reminds me that we are not at the end of the therapy just because he is coming home. He will continue to get stronger every week, yes, but it will be slow.

I feel more anxiety over what I don't know. What I do know I feel very good about.

This weekend will be very busy as I tie up loose ends, continue to practice activities of daily living with Bob, and prepare for my business trip to Dallas on Monday. I will return Wednesday night so I can go with him to his surgery Thursday. I will resume work on Friday, but then, once he is discharged, I am planning to take a week off to give us a chance to get settled and figure out our new routine.

Assuming all goes well, Bob should be sleeping in our bed again by around October 12. That will be five months from when this all started. Semper avanti.

Thursday, October 9, 2014

The surgery went beautifully; the bone flap fit perfectly. Calling to mind the movie *Young Frankenstein* again, I am relieved to learn we have no Abby Normal to worry about. Bob is in recovery, so I still have to wait to see him. The anesthesia often causes the patient to regress a little, but he should be back to where he was prior to the surgery in a couple of days. He may be coming home on Saturday.

Saturday, October 11, 2014

The post-op pain is worse than either of us expected, but despite that, Bob's progress is good. They had to cut jaw muscle and move his eye temporarily during the surgery, so he has additional pain besides the incision. None of that is considered out of the ordinary, but we just had no idea (thank God). Anyway, the PEG tube came out yesterday, and the head drain came out today. For the first time in five months, Bob has no tubes sticking out of his head or body!

During an assessment today Bob was able to move the middle finger of his right hand. We agreed that could come in handy.

The medical center is very dreary compared to the rehab center. Bob's window literally looks out to a concrete wall, and the noise level is very high. While we were there today, some man was yelling, "Give me my goddamn money!" We wondered whether he was a patient or someone from the finance office.

We are hoping for discharge Sunday, but no one is really saying. I guess they will decide when they decide, and we'll know when they decide. Unfortunately for me, it isn't until today that I realize I have been taking the long way to the parking garage every day. I so can't wait for this part to be over!

Sunday, October 12, 2014

Today is the five-month anniversary of Bob's stroke. I had my hopes pinned on bringing him home today, in large part due to the expectations set by the rehab team, the surgeon, and even the resident yesterday who removed the head drain and said Sunday looked likely for discharge. But today when Julia and I arrive, we learn that the physical therapy department needs to make the determination as to whether he should go home or go to rehab, and they won't see him until tomorrow. *Aack!* Pour me another vodka tonic! I need to keep reminding myself that I control nothing. Just because I go out and get a bouquet of Mylar balloons, a big Welcome Home banner, and a beautiful flower arrangement doesn't mean the hospital is going to cooperate. Can you get Mylar balloons refilled? What a horrible homecoming—imagine being greeted by shriveled balloons drooping on the floor, looking worse than you do. I don't think so.

As for the good news, Bob looks even better today, and he says his head pain is almost gone. So, not to be selfish, but my plan of having this week without an alarm clock or a schedule and just letting us figure ourselves out for seven days feels very much in jeopardy. I need to be at the hospital tomorrow at 9:00 a.m. sharp, to make sure I am there when rounds are done, so I can get the doctors, therapists, Bob, and me all on the same page.

Bob said it best: the closer he gets to getting home, the longer it seems to take.

Monday, October 13, 2014

During physical therapy this morning we agree that Bob needs another day to build back his strength for transfers, so discharge looks like Tuesday, and we are still tracking to go home. We get permission to go off the floor, and we tour the hospital just for a change in scenery. Have wheelchair, will travel.

We are both trying hard not to view this delay as a setback but rather as expectations having been set too high. His head pain is gone and he is getting stronger, so progress is continuing. Semper avanti.

Tuesday, October 14, 2014

We are home! We were ready to leave around two o'clock this afternoon but did not get our clearance until quarter after six. We had to wait an extra hour while the hospital staff wrote out all the prescriptions for the so-called home meds. They resisted, telling me they had but one prescription and the rest were home meds. "But he hasn't been home for five months," I argued. "We don't have any of these." It was a circular argument, with them not wanting to write prescriptions for home meds and me pointing out that Bob hasn't been home. But we got it resolved, and we are home. We have dinner together and watch the Kansas City Royals play the Baltimore Orioles. It is overwhelming. We are exhausted. We are relieved. We are blessed. Our next phase starts tomorrow. Semper avanti.

Thursday, October 16, 2014

A friend once said we'd experience a roller-coaster ride of euphoria and despair, euphoria and despair. The past two days have been like that. I don't think I could have been any more prepared for Bob's return, and yet so many little things caught me off guard—like just how hard it is to push a transport chair around a carpeted bedroom and down a hallway. It took two and a half hours Tuesday night to get ready for bed.

Our first morning together we were so spent that we greeted the visiting nurse and physical therapist in our pajamas—and it was eleven thirty. Physical therapy workers put us through our paces but determined we were doing everything safely. We went out in the rain, hoping to get a new transport chair. Despite the fact that I had to drape Bob in an old Girl Scout poncho to get him out of the house and to the car, he couldn't help but exclaim what a beautiful day it was as we drove through West Chester. We had no luck with the chair, but we did score two Capriotti subs on our way back home with which to watch the end of the American League baseball game. We happily cheered on the Kansas City Royals. It has been fun to follow all our former Blue Rocks players into the Show.

Today Bob and I are thinking of attending my professional association's fortieth anniversary semiformal gala event at the Springfield Country Club. I am on the board, and we've called the event "Delaware Valley HIMSS: Forty and Fabulous!" because we felt that this was an occasion to celebrate. HIMSS was founded in 1961, so we are one of the early chapters. What started as a group of thirty engineers from Pennsylvania Hospital back in 1974 now has a nineteen-hundred-plus membership covering eastern Pennsylvania, Delaware, and South Jersey. HIMSS stands for Healthcare Information Management Systems and Society, and this event celebrating our chapter's contributions to HIMSS has been in the works for a year. In my mind, attending this dinner will be a milestone of sorts. After five long months of seemingly endless hospitals and rehab, I hope getting dressed up and going to this dinner-dance will somehow make all the hard work worth it; it will be an indication that, slowly but surely, we are in fact getting our life back.

As if to save ourselves for the event, we keep today very low key. We do not go anywhere. I help Bob shower and give him an actual traditional shave. He falls asleep in the recliner for two hours, and I do some odds and ends of office work. At four o'clock we are not exhausted, so we decide to give it a try. By six o'clock I am in my sparkly dress, Bob is in his dark suit with an open-collared shirt and Chaddsford Planning baseball cap, and we are headed to Springfield. It is a great opener for this home phase: dinner and socializing with colleagues and friends in an elegant setting. Semper avanti.

Monday, October 20, 2014

Today I reflect back that Benjamin Robert Bucceri came into this world on October 20, 1994, hands first. That should have been a clue right then and there that our Benny was going to insist on doing things his way. While Julia reminds me of her father, Ben takes more after me. He doesn't get why pure logic often doesn't win the argument, and he isn't above getting himself into just a little bit of trouble. But the bane of Ben's existence growing up was Lisa. To most people, Lisa was an American Girl doll. But to Julia, Lisa was her sister. This, of course, drove Ben nuts. "She's a *doll*!" he would yell as he threw up his six-year-old hands in disgust. One day I found Lisa in the mailbox.

While Julia had been a GIFT from science, Ben had been a gift from nature. It was the winter of 1994, and we had just come home from an afternoon of cross-country skiing. It was an uncharacteristically miserable day, because I loved cross-country skiing. Bob asked me what was wrong, and I said, "I don't know. I haven't been this tired since—*gasp!*" And our beautiful Ben was born eight months later. He weighed ten pounds and had a thick head of long, jet-black hair that brushed his collar. People visiting the nursery commented on how adorable the three-month old Mexican baby was.

I thought about how Bob's father had never gotten to see Bob turn twenty and I think what a blessing it was that Bob was here for Ben. Bob's father had died when Bob was nineteen years old. It was one of the reasons he worked so hard to keep himself fit, and it was not lost on me that Ben was nineteen the day Bob had his stroke.

So here we are, five months later. Figuring out the new normal takes time, and some days have been better than others. But the bottom line is that it is getting worked out. Home health care is set up for three days a week, and we can spread out the visits so that someone comes every day: the nurse, the physical therapist, the personal aid, or the occupational therapist. But it quickly becomes apparent that those visits are too short and infrequent; they are not enough to provide Bob with the attention and care he needs while I go in to the office every day. One afternoon, while I am on the phone, Bob completely flips over his wheelchair and lands on the hardwood floor. It takes an hour and a lot of ingenuity to get him off the floor and back in the chair. So we will need a private duty nurse, weekdays from eight in the morning until four in the afternoon. My goal is to have that person get him ready and out the door to rehab for outpatient therapy when that begins.

All in all, the weekend was good. We celebrated Ben's birthday on the weekend. He and Bob went together to West Side Little League to take in a game and visit with some neighborhood friends. We went to Mass, did our Sunday grocery shopping routine, and then celebrated Ben's birthday with his specially requested spicy fried chicken, mashed potatoes, roasted asparagus, and chocolate birthday cake. It was beautiful in its simplicity.

Friday, October 24, 2014

The week was not without its trials and tribulations, but restless nights and adjustment challenges notwithstanding, Bob and I end the week on a high note. We decide to celebrate all we have accomplished these past ten days and test the restaurant waters in West Chester. So dinner out it is. Therapy has progressed to the point where Bob did some limited walking with the brace today. The full-time caregiver came Wednesday and brought great relief to me, among other things.

It is a little trying for Bob to have a caregiver who wants to be his new best friend, but I knew I had made the right decision to bring on full-time help when he fell out of his wheelchair. Possibly the seminal moment of the week was when the nurse took the stitches out of his head and the incision began to resemble a part in his hair rather than the Frankenstein zipper scar it had been. Or maybe it was putting on a pair of cords today, with a real fly. He told the caregiver, "I want to wear big-boy pants today." I guess he's had his fill of elastic-waist workout pants.

Among the nicest parts of the week were two visits: one from Fritz who came over to watch a few World Series innings, and one from a colleague and friend of Bob's, George who continued the weekly visits he started back in June, bringing Bob a fresh cup of coffee and some interesting conversation. Since we hadn't left the house since Sunday evening, except for one quick errand I ran during lunchtime the first day we had the caregiver, having visitors was such a treat.

This weekend brings with it more West Side baseball, more World Series games, and prep for our impending trip to Florida— wardrobe prep, that is. We managed to get him into a suit forty-eight hours out of the hospital, so we know at least one suit fits. And I guess I'd better google how to tie a half Windsor. Semper avanti.

Friday, October 31, 2014

We continue to march toward our goal of attending the EBT Next Generation conference in Florida. The care team has been very supportive of our goal and spends a good amount of time with us going over our air-travel strategy, logistics, and game plan to help make sure we have covered all the bases.

Bob had his first visit with our primary-care doctor since all this happened. He trusts her and was anxious to have his care turned back over to her after the past five months. She had been consulted back in May and had been getting copies of result reports along the way, so we had kept her well informed. It was quite a homecoming. She was so happy to see him and so amazed at how well he was doing. She told Bob that she had talked to the neurosurgeon in Virginia and been shocked at what had happened, given how well Bob had taken care of himself. She said when she'd heard he was coming in this week she'd been full of apprehension as to who she'd meet. She took Bob's hand in hers and said, "I can't tell you how happy I am that it is *you!*" He became very emotional; we both knew what she meant. It was such a celebration.

Home therapy and the visiting nurse have been wonderful. Today Bob was officially discharged from the home-based care because of the anticipated trip out of state, and next Friday marks the start of outpatient therapy.

I am fully adjusted to our weekday caregiver. I call her a godsend, but Bob would probably call her a necessary evil. She is competent and good-hearted, and respectful. And she is willing to let him do things that I probably would be reluctant to, only because I am a risk-averse wife. But I am preparing to leave him to her care and other caregivers for a week in mid-November when I go to Dallas, and I want to make sure she knows that while he is currently disabled with a brain injury that is still healing, he is no child. It came up quite naturally, about how easy it is to start looking at someone as a child when you have to wipe his bottom. So today she and I had a talk about the competent, intelligent, and strong man that she is helping recover from a very bad hit.

We close the week with some travel prep. Bob goes to get his hair cut, and I take advantage of the caregiver's presence and go to get my nails done. Bob's first trip to the barber is another homecoming of sorts, and he loves not only getting the haircut but the social aspect of going to the barber again and catching up on borough news. It is quite an ordeal getting him up the step into the old brick building, but the barber and some strapping young customers lift the chair into the shop. His hair is all one length now and he looks much more like his old self.

The only real downside to the week is that the Royals lose the World Series. But it was exciting and a great run. About a hundred days until pitchers and catchers report, and the Blue Rocks schedule arrived just yesterday.

Thursday, November 6, 2014

On Tuesday, November 4, Bob was honored with the establishment of the annual Robert A. Bucceri Leadership Award during the seventeenth annual EBT Next Generation conference in Clearwater, Florida. It was a very proud moment for both of us. The fact that he was there in person to accept the award was thrilling. It was not too long ago that the idea of Bob making the trip was unthinkable. Gradually it became a stretch goal, then it became possible, and eventually, with support from friends and Bob's care team, we gained the confidence and courage to just do it.

My assumption all along was that we'd make the trip for the luncheon and awards ceremony: one night, in and out. Fool that I was! Two and a half weeks ago, when we'd decided it was a go and I had gone to make the flight arrangements, he'd insisted we attend the whole conference. *His* assumption all along had been that it was all or nothing. He was one of the organizers, he argued. He needed to be there for the whole thing. And so we were.

Any thoughts that we were crazy to make the trip just three weeks after Bob's return from over five months of hospitalization were quickly put to rest. The warm welcome and genuine friendship and respect that I witnessed toward Bob from his colleagues—and these are competitors, as well as public-sector customers, who often strive to keep a cordial distance from their private-sector vendors—was so heartwarming to me. It was better than any therapy that could have been prescribed.

Along the way I learned a lot about the electronic payments industry. I got to meet the people I had heard about for so many years. I got to meet the woman that saved Bob's life. I got to see a whole room full of people—more than three hundred—honor my husband *twice* with a standing ovation. The trip exceeded my expectations and confirmed for me once again that I should never underestimate the man to whom I am married. Semper avanti.

Wednesday, November 12, 2014

Our weekend was quiet and uneventful, except for the joyride in Bob's truck. It is an F-150 and quite high, so it was no small feat for Bob to climb into and out of the truck. What surprised me was that in some ways it was easier than the Honda CR-V. Now we can take our truck out when we want, and so we do.

The weekend was capped with visits from neighbors and dinner with friends on Sunday. It couldn't have been nicer.

I am now in Dallas, Texas, on business for the week. Bob and I are both uncomfortable with having a private-duty caregiver in the house while he sleeps at night. Hopefully we will both get used to it, because it will be necessary until he is independent.

Outpatient therapy begins for Bob this week. He had his assessment last Friday and came home, once again, impressed with the rehab and anxious to get started. There is a lot the team wants to do to help him alleviate the pain in his right arm and leg and continue his progress toward walking. The schedule this week is two 5-hour days. A CAT scan is needed Wednesday in preparation for the follow-up visit to the neurosurgeon next week. A friend is coming to have dinner with Bob Thursday, so hopefully the week will be busy enough to go fast until I get home Friday evening.

The next milestone we have been looking forward to is Thanksgiving. We usually host cousins from Bob's side and their families, and we are hoping this year will be no different. We are so looking forward to it, so glad our cousins can make the trip.

Next Thursday, November 20, our friends have organized a happy hour at Barnaby's restaurant in West Chester as a kind of welcome-home party for Bob. We do feel like partying after everything we have been through and all that Bob has accomplished. I had thought of doing an open house to invite all the people who have been sending us cards, notes, dinners, and other support. Once I started to think it through, I realized I had finally found my limit. But my good friend Nancy once again stepped in to rescue me from myself and suggested the happy hour.

Bob continues to get stronger, and we are hopeful and optimistic about his continued recovery. Life is good. Semper avanti.

Sunday, November 16, 2014

My trip to Texas was uneventful, though things were not so uneventful on Bob's end. Everything seemed to be going well, I thought—until I received a call from him at seven thirty Friday morning, telling me that he had fallen and hit his head while trying to get to the bathroom. The overnight caregiver had not heard his calls, and so he'd decided to take matters into his own hands. When I realized where he had fallen I was impressed—he'd gotten pretty far! He must have walked about five feet before his right knee buckled. It was a long day for him, involving yet another CAT scan, but luckily no harm had been done. Despite the ordeal, he managed to greet me with a vase of long-stemmed red roses to welcome me home. My heart just melted.

Ben came home this weekend, so Bob had a football buddy and exercise partner. Bob got a whole new set of exercises at therapy, so they spent almost an hour working through them all together. Ben knew exactly how to do the stretches and did a great job. I called them my gym rats, and they seemed to enjoy the label.

Bob's therapists are confident they can get the right leg stronger so he can walk. They are more concerned about the right arm, the fact that his fingers are starting to curl, and the constant shoulder pain. We have to schedule an x-ray, and in the meantime Bob has a new splint for his wrist and hand to help keep it from curling. More Botox will be injected in multiple places.

He is also engaging in therapy to help him get back to work. This man is not interested in using this stroke as a reason to retire. Semper avanti.

Sunday, November 23, 2014

This was another big week. First Bob had his follow-up visit with the neurosurgeon and received a good report. The surgery itself was a great success, with everything healed well and no indications of any issues in the latest CAT scan. There were a couple of take-aways. First, an MRI will be needed in February to check the growth of the tumor on the pituitary gland. The surgeon reminded us that it is not a small tumor; it bears watching because it is close to the optic nerve and could impact Bob's vision at some point. It was not removed because it wasn't hurting anything, it would have meant serious brain surgery, and frankly, Bob's brain had been through enough trauma already. The surgeon's rationale made sense to both of us. The second take-away was that Bob can be weaned off the anti-seizure medicine, so we are starting that this week. He will have a small chance of a seizure for the rest of his life, but he hasn't had any yet, so the surgeon said the need for the medicine as a preemptive measure has really passed.

All that said, Bob was cautioned that alcohol could trigger a seizure, so the advice was to stay away from it or indulge in just one drink for special occasions.

I once witnessed a seizure, and it was very scary. It was Holy Thursday, 2006, a week after my father had died. I was executrix of his estate, so I had set up a meeting with an attorney in town who had been referred to me but whom I had never met. The attorney smiled as we greeted and shook hands and then, strangely, motioned for me to sit on the coffee table in the reception area. He started talking in gibberish, peppered with an occasionally audible "Oh my God." As it turned out, he was having a stroke. Within minutes he had a grand mal seizure. Happily he survived, made a full recovery, and I went on to hire him as my parents' estate attorney, but it was terrifying just the same.

This week was also marked by two social events that were very special. First was the happy hour at Barnaby's. Bob and I both got a chance to spend some social time with friends from our neighborhood, church, Bob's business, and West Side Little League.

The second was on Saturday night to mark the end of the Coach Bob Swings for Recovery event several of our friends organized and West Side Little League sponsored. There was a raffle, candy sales at baseball games, a pizza night, and Thursday's happy hour, all intended to provide a way for people to help Bob in his time of need. Saturday night there was a gathering of the planning committee and other participants, which marked the end of the raffle with me blindly drawing the names of the winners and Bob reading them off. It was a fun night that we will never forget. We were deeply moved by it all, knowing the planning and work that must have gone into it on top of the existing demands on our friends. We will never really know who participated, but we are grateful to and thankful for everyone who sold or bought raffle tickets, bought candy or pizza, or gave their time and resources to help make it happen. We are so blessed. How did we ever get so lucky as to have such a huge support system behind us?

We don't know how long Bob will be in therapy or how long he will be in recovery and require the support of a caregiver. He is making so much progress. His legs are getting stronger every day, but it is a long, slow slog. And we don't know how long "long" will be. The Coach Bob Swings for Recovery event will go a long way to help us get Bob the resources he will need.

Friday, November 28, 2014

◇◇◇◇

This week marked another milestone we had been looking forward to for the past several months. We have had much to be thankful for coming into this holiday, and we were blessed with a house full of cousins and their children, in addition to our own children, who came home from college. From Tuesday dinner through breakfast this morning our home was filled with lots of noisy conversation and laughter. It was not unlike most

Thanksgivings at our house, and I took comfort in that sameness. The only things different were that Bob and his cousins did not end up in the basement checking out all Bob's fly fishing equipment and I made the Thanksgiving turkey gravy. I am a good cook, but gravy is Bob's turf. My plan was to have him stand at the stove and make it himself, because he has gotten very good with balance over the past couple of weeks, but he was so involved in his visiting that I ended up just taking my chances and trying it myself.

Two inches of snowfall on Wednesday gave us a taste of what winter will be like, and I did not enjoy it, beautiful as it was. The ramps that have made the house accessible from the deck were covered in snow, and where the flagstone walk meets the driveway, it is uneven and difficult to negotiate with snow on the ground. Bob's cousin Ernie spent the day installing handrails at the garage steps, and his timing could not have been better. I had been thinking that we were at least a few weeks away from Bob really being able to use them, but damn if that man did not insist on giving it a try after we got home from therapy today.

I put the transport chair at the base of the steps in the garage, stood on the steps, and then pulled Bob's wheelchair to the door opening. He stood on the top step and, with me providing some guidance to his right foot, stepped down to the garage floor, pivoted, and sat in the transport chair. *Voila!* We then reversed the process and went up the three steps. The metal threshold was a little tricky, but we figured it out, and in the wheelchair he went.

He may never let me wheel him out the back door again. Semper avanti.

Sunday, November 30, 2014

A little over a week before our trip to Florida, we had received an invitation in the mail to a surprise birthday party for my aunt Judie on November 29. At the time I was not sure Florida would work, but I had quickly contacted my cousin to let her know. If we could fly to

Florida three weeks after Bob's hospitalization I reasoned a two and a half hour drive to Cape May, New Jersey after six weeks would be a snap. Our answer to the invitation at the time had been a definite maybe, but as soon as we returned from Florida I told my cousin we would be there, and so would our children.

The logistics of the surprise were well executed. It is hard to duck behind anything when you are in or pushing a wheelchair, but we managed to check in to the hotel with my aunt being ushered around by her granddaughter less than fifty feet away without ever getting caught! There were twenty-some family members altogether, and only five were supposed to be there for the "girls' weekend" that was the pretense for the event.

We stayed at an historic inn, Congress Hall, which originally opened in 1816. It was officially equipped with an ADA-approved room, but the old thresholds, uneven floors, and extra louvered door in front of every room made maneuvering a little challenging. Some of the floors actually slanted, so I found myself pushing uphill to go down the hall. I have never been sensitive to these kinds of things before, but pushing a wheelchair certainly heightens awareness of even the smallest details. Don't get me wrong; we loved the inn. But we are learning what it means to travel with a physical disability and what "ADA compliant" actually means.

We dressed for dinner and left ahead of the appointed time, to make sure we could take the extra time a wheelchair and car transfers demand without risking the surprise. This was to be a dressy occasion, so Julia and I were in evening dresses and heels and Bob and Ben were handsome in suits and ties. After all, how many times does one celebrate a seventy-fifth birthday? I am sure the look on my face when we arrived at our dinner destination was priceless. Across the sprawling, rolling lawn, up two long sets of concrete stairs, sat the Peter Shields Inn—beautiful and stately on a hill as it overlooked the Atlantic Ocean across the street. *Oy.*

I knew before the hostess confirmed it that there was no entrance that did not involve copious numbers of stairs. Thank God for a strong, strapping son and even stronger, strappier male cousins. Bob was carried up those stairs as if the wheelchair were a litter and he was the goddamn king of Siam! Everyone at the inn made the extra effort to accommodate Bob's chair, so it all worked out in the end. The inn was beautiful, and the evening was very special. As Bob said later on, it was the kind of night you wished would never end. But like all good things, it did end, and we crashed into bed exhausted but so glad we had made the trip and been able to share in the special night.

Tuesday, December 9, 2014

It is about five in the morning, and I have finally decided to get up. Bob woke me at 3:15 to help him pee, which is fairly routine, but this morning I had trouble falling back to sleep. A lot has been weighing on my mind this past week. Bob completed his first three-day week of outpatient therapy at the rehab, and it went well but left him spent for other things. His ambitions to get back into even a little bit of work have been tempered by his exhaustion. The physical demands of being his right arm and right leg have been taking their toll on me as well. At times I feel we are taking "two steps forward, one step back." While it is true that we have been exclusively using the garage steps to get in and out of the house, I have found myself doing more lifting lately to help him in and out of a chair. It seemed in mid-November that he had progressed to the point where I basically served as spotter for certain chair transfers, but that seems to have diminished. Apparently this is to be expected—at least that is what the therapists say. The three-day outpatient program is quite aggressive, and it sometimes takes several weeks for the patient's brain to adjust to all the work. So it is mental exhaustion that continues for Bob and physical exhaustion for me.

What weighs on me is wondering how I will be able to keep the pace up. When this all started, I did not know what I did not know, so I was able to sustain myself partly because of naïveté and partly because I am a positive person at heart and a person of faith. I knew back in the summer that, as hard as it was then, the real hard work would come when Bob came home. I didn't know what that really meant, though, so it remained an abstract thought, and I had been able to push it aside until now. After almost two months, the hard work is taking its toll on my neck and arms, so I am hoping a few sessions with the chiropractor will help alleviate that. I think my six foot height contributes to the problem, because of the constant bending and stooping, so I am looking for alternative ways to accomplish the tasks at hand that don't put such a strain on my neck. Having the caregiver is a huge blessing, because it relieves me of the physical demands of caring for Bob during the workday. But I am still going into the workweek exhausted and aching, so the worry about sustaining the job is weighing on me as well.

In the meantime, Bob continues his hard work and positive attitude. He is frustrated at the slow pace, which I can fully appreciate, but he continues to make progress. He is on fewer medications than when he was an inpatient, so that is another good sign. I know he worries about me, as I worry about him. He wants desperately to help when he suggests that he run upstairs and get the transport chair for me. The therapists are not surprised at this either, telling me it can take a long time for his brain to synchronize what it thinks he can do with what he can actually do. When Bob says things like that, I just give him a look, and he eventually realizes the mistake. "I know," he says with a sigh. "If I could get the transport chair for you, we wouldn't need the transport chair."

I know we will figure it all out. It's all still good, and every day is a day together that we shouldn't have but do. But it is hard, and it would be dishonest to pretend there aren't days when I wish I could crawl under the covers and hide. Semper avanti.

Wednesday, December 10, 2014

Yesterday I attended a team meeting at the rehab center with Bob and his caregiver. There was so much positive news and such optimism from the team that it really helped me adjust my mind-set. On the good side, the whole team is seeing a big increase in Bob's focus, concentration, and endurance. On the down side, his arm and shoulder are a very big challenge, and the occupational therapist said that, even taking the stroke out of the equation, the orthopedic issues are challenging. She remained optimistic that a lot can be done, but she admitted she cannot focus on mobility and function until she can address the pain and range of motion. The whole team was very happy to hear that we do exercises on the off days, because they do think that will help a lot. It is rare for a patient to do that, they said, so we felt we had gotten a gold star from the teacher.

Interestingly, once the physical therapist heard that Bob was using the garage steps to access the house, he quickly changed his therapy plan to focus on that. The big leg brace that was made for Bob is still just used in therapy, so we now can use it as a knee immobilizer to wrap around the leg and help stabilize the knee when we do the stairs at home. We can also use it to do standing exercises around the house. I like the fact that, rather than reprimanding us for going off plan and taking a risk, the therapist is keeping up with us, working to our plan, and helping us make sure we are doing what we want safely.

We also got into a group discussion about Bob's impulsive behavior. It is a double-edged sword. He is getting stronger and feeling better, so he tries new things, but he often tries them without me or the caregiver or wants to try them when we are in the middle of something else. It scares the hell out of us. The caregiver talked about her challenge of keeping him safe without making him mad, and not wanting to get into an argument with him. He talked about how he needs to be able to advance. He made the point that he has been working so hard all these months, and he wants to put what he has been working on in therapy into practice at home. I piped in with my wifely comments, and together the therapists knew just how to handle us. They got Bob to agree to try to communicate to us ahead of time that he wants to stretch his skills but to understand that we will always put his safety first. And we recognized that his risk taking is a natural part of his progress. I know there will still be issues, but at least we each know how the others feel now.

Today's big excitement is the delivery of our new snow blower. Bob and I have always liked shoveling, for the most part, but I know I can't handle it now with everything else, and I don't want any barriers to getting him to therapy. So I started looking for someone to plow us out. I have come up zero in finding someone who will do residential driveways. Everyone is getting out of the business or only doing commercial properties. So we did some research, and Bob and I went out in the pouring rain on Saturday and picked out a snow blower. Now, let's hope we don't get any snow this winter. I only sort of want to play with my new toy.

Wednesday, December 24, 2014

There have been some breakthroughs over the past ten days, one of which is the range of motion in Bob's arm and the therapist's declaration on Monday that he has regained over 80 percent functionality. What that means is that his arm can be manipulated to do most of the movements it could do before the event in May. What is still missing is the brain connection that directs the arm movements, but the improvement in the range of motion is big; it's a prerequisite to ever getting the arm or hand to work again in any meaningful way.

Another breakthrough has been some increased walking at home. Bob's impulsiveness has become dangerous, because he is now strong enough to act on those impulses. He has fallen several times over the past month because of it, one fall being a very public sprawl in the parking lot of a restaurant where we were meeting friends for dinner before a Christmas concert. I was getting the wheelchair out of the trunk, and Bob decided to get out of the car. Luckily, no harm was done, except for a marble-sized bump on his right elbow, so we could laugh about it while I scolded him. The last thing he needs is a sprained knee, twisted ankle, or broken bone to set his rehab back by months. He knows this, but at the same time he often does not remember that he still needs assistance.

To try to head him off at the pass, I got him a quad cane, or a "grandpa cane," as he calls it. So with my help on the right and the cane on the left, he can start doing some simple steps besides the ones that take him in and out of the garage. For the past couple of days we have been parking the wheelchair outside the powder room, and he has been taking steps with the cane in his left hand and my guidance and support on the right to go into the bathroom. His right foot tends to splay out to the right, so I have to help stabilize it by pointing his foot forward sometimes, but he is taking steps just the same, and they are becoming a little more natural as he goes. This is all probably highly illegal where the therapists are concerned, because he is not wearing his leg brace when we are doing these things, but it is becoming increasingly difficult to hold the man back.

As for the impulsiveness, I have trained myself to remind him when I need to leave the room or turn my back that he is to stay where he is until I return. No funny stuff. In the loving way that only I can say it, I tell him that if he tries to get up without me he is dead meat.

He gets angry with me if he feels I am holding him back or coddling him. Some days I am not as patient or sympathetic as I should be, those mostly being days when I am at my most tired and he wants things done a certain way and immediately. It is part of the impulsiveness that he does not realize he is being demanding, and I do not always hide my frustration well. On a recent Sunday morning we decided to luxuriate in the supermarket cafe with our coffees and mini pastries after our weekly grocery shopping. It was such a lovely little respite from our day. I got a little emotional at one point, realizing I'd be lost without him. So I told him, and I asked him to remember that the next time I got impatient or cross. Later on that day he referred to me as his "sweetness." Was he being sarcastic? I asked. "No," he said with a laugh, "never!"

So here we are, Christmas Eve. Bob and I were up at the crack of dawn to get him to therapy, and it rained all day. But just as Bob, Julia, Ben, and I headed to Mass, the rain tapered off and made it easy on us. We had a beautiful dinner together that lasted almost two hours because of all the conversations we got into. While I occasionally mourn the loss of the life we had together before May 12, tonight, this most holy night, I am reminded of the gift of family that we do have, and I am very happy.

Wednesday, December 31, 2014

The year 2014 cannot end quickly enough for me. I do not want to reflect on the good and bad, the losses in our family, the blessings of Bob's survival and progress toward recovery. I just want to put it all behind me, get the hell out of 2014, continue to move forward and toast the arrival of 2015 in anticipation of a good year. Semper avanti.

Thursday, January 1, 2015

Today was a beautiful, sunny, cold day with the high about thirty-nine degrees. Bob had been offering to go on my walk with me for a couple of weeks, so today I thought, *Why not?* As usual, I was an enthusiastic supporter of the idea but had fairly low expectations. I loaded the transport chair into the car, along with the quad cane and knee immobilizer, assuming we'd get maybe one hundred feet before he'd be spent and I'd need to wheel him back to the car.

We drove over to our local park, where for the past ten years Bob has spent the spring and summer coaching baseball. As usual, I'd underestimated just what Bob could do. We walked from the car all the way up the sloping sidewalk to the baseball field, rested against the retaining wall for about five minutes, and then made our way back. I don't know how far it is, exactly, maybe four hundred feet? The wheelchair never came out of the car. Bob's right knee and ankle were wrapped in immobilizing braces, and he had the quad cane on his left. I guided on the right, sometimes lifting the right leg and prompting it forward but many times just giving it verbal cues or no cue at all. About ten feet from the end of our round trip, his right hip just stopped cooperating, as if to say, "I have done enough for today." We attempted to sit on a nearby bench but instead fell into it, a tangled mess of limbs and cane, with Bob on top of me. Not a dignified way to end the walk, but as Bob said, you don't know how far is too far until you reach it. And our course was only about ten feet too long. No lasting harm was done, and it was exhilarating to be out in the brisk, cold air and sunshine. We are now appropriately exhausted. The whole exercise took over an hour, but it felt great, especially to Bob who has not walked outside like that since May 11, 2014. I am very happy that 2015 got to be the year to mark this milestone walk. Semper avanti.

Photo Gallery

Our favorite family vacation, Hawaii, 2005

Henry's Fork, Idaho fishing trip, July 27, 2013

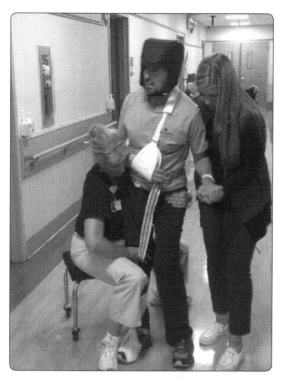

Learning to stand up and walk again in acute
inpatient rehab, August 16, 2014

Bob and Nancy in Cape May, New Jersey, November 29, 2014

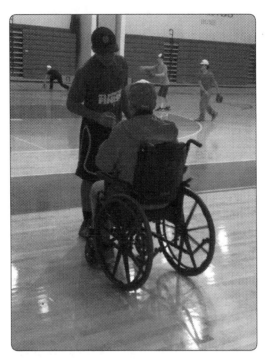

Bob working with a pitcher, February 20, 2015

Game Day, April 1, 2015

Presenting "Trouble with the Curve" to the Delaware Valley
HIMSS group, Citizen's Bank Park, Philadelphia, May 11, 2015

Strategies for Getting from One Day to the Next

Friends and family alike often asked me during those first eight months how I was managing so well. At first I was so close to it that I could not see what I was doing. I had no clue whether I was managing well or managing badly. In my mind, I was just getting up every day and trying to survive. So I started thinking about it, and I realized there were strategies to survival that I had formed in my own head as I was going through each day and trying to make sure I got to the next one. Some of the strategies came from advice I was getting from loved ones. Some were inspired by the kindness we were receiving from friends, even ones whom we had lost touch with prior to the stroke. Some of the strategies came from my years of business experience as a problem solver, and I guess some of them came from my personality. I have always been basically positive, believing that every problem has a solution. I am a "glass half full" kind of girl, but I came to realize there was a lot more to my survival than just being optimistic.

There are actually ten strategies I use on a regular basis. I say "use," because this struggle has not ended. It may never end, and in some ways, as Bob progresses it gets harder. Except for the first strategy, these are in no particular order. To this day I employ them dynamically, as needed, and sometimes simultaneously. On really bad days I draw on every last one.

Strategy 1: Take a deep breath

> *Your breathing is your greatest friend. Return to it in all your troubles and you will find comfort and guidance.*
>
> —Anonymous

This is my first strategy, because it really was the first thing I did. Women who have gone through labor and delivery will get this immediately. There is a lot of research to back up the healthful benefits of breathing purposefully and deeply. In fact, besides everything I ever learned in childbirth class, I found there are eighteen benefits to deep, abdominal breathing that go beyond stress relief. These include improved digestion, removal of toxins, improved posture, more efficient cellular regeneration, and a stronger heart, to name just a few. Who knew? Breathing deeply encourages full oxygen exchange—that is, the beneficial trade of incoming oxygen for outgoing carbon dioxide. Not surprisingly, it can slow the heartbeat and lower or stabilize blood pressure. That is what it did for me that night when I got the first call from the hospital.

This strategy is beautiful in its simplicity but somewhat unnatural to do, so it takes some practice. Here are three easy steps:

1. Inhale through your nose, expanding your belly and then filling your chest for a count of five.

2. Hold, and count to three.

3. Exhale fully from slightly opened mouth, counting to five.

I began regularly and consciously using this strategy as early as day three. That was when the enormity of the situation really began to sink in, the business of getting to Virginia was done, and the emotional impact of my husband's strong prospects of a grim future started to well up inside. I actually received coaching from a nurse friend of mine as I sobbed into the phone over worries about our nineteen-year-old son. He was alone at home in Pennsylvania, while I was in Virginia, unable to see how he was coping. I had chest pains and shortness of breath. I thought I was having a heart attack. She helped me do breathing exercises to relieve my stress, and they really worked. I used them again and again until it became almost a ritual exercise for me each morning as I awoke to the realization that this wasn't a nightmare, it was my life.

While I did not adopt deep breathing as a deliberate strategy until day three, in the beginning I instinctively took simple deep breaths just as a stall tactic to help me think of my next step. After the initial call from the hospital's social worker on May 12, I would stop and take a deep breath to give me a chance to get my head on straight as I went from conversation to conversation. I would hear what the social worker was telling me. I would hear what the doctor was saying, but it wasn't really sinking in. After approving the surgery that was Bob's only hope for survival, not knowing what else to say, I stated the obvious. "I guess I need to come there."

"Yes," said the doctor patiently. "That would be good."

I immediately sought out my new boss to ask for help getting a flight to Washington, DC, as soon as possible, but after that I was lost. What would I tell our children? What would I have them do? Should I tell them to go to Virginia? Stay where they were and await more news? Could it really, possibly, be this serious? Who else should I call? I ended up calling Bob's cousin Ernie, a former U.S. Marine. He helped me stay calm and formulate what to tell the kids, and then he took on the job of notifying other family members for me. And I called my good friend and neighbor, Nancy, just so someone in the neighborhood would know what was happening. Our son was alone, so I wanted someone nearby to know. She didn't hesitate to tell me she'd be picking Ben up within fifteen minutes to take him to Virginia. The kids would have an experienced adult and family friend with them at the hospital until I could get there. On top of that, she insisted on picking me up at Reagan International Airport the very next morning. She was, and is, an amazing friend.

Strategy 2: Own your happiness

If you want to live a happy life. tie it to a goal, not to people or objects.

—Albert Einstein, physicist

Happiness is not something that happens *to* you. It is a choice. I learned this long ago, when I was in my twenties and Bob and I had been struggling with infertility for several years. It was my first exposure to just how little I really controlled in life, and it threatened our marriage, because I could not accept the idea that I might not be able to have any children. My life seemed over. Then a counselor said to me, "So, in other words, you are not going to allow yourself to be happy." It stopped me in my tracks, and I protested that this was not my fault. But as we talked some more, I realized that what this person was saying made so much sense. I was defining my life and what would make it happy in very narrow terms. In effect, rather than owning my own happiness, I was setting myself up for misery.

It was a turning point for me, and I became determined that our infertility would strengthen our marriage and that I would find alternative paths to happiness. German philosopher Friedrich Nietzsche once wrote, "That which does not destroy me, makes me stronger."

Our experience with infertility did strengthen me, and both Bob and I used the experience to strengthen our marriage. I knew couples that had split over it, and I was determined not to let that happen to us.

Years later we were blessed with two beautiful children, and wouldn't you know it, I often heard myself explaining to them during their own trials and tribulations that, while they couldn't control everything that happened to them, they could control how they responded to it. Along with that came the lesson that they had to own their own happiness.

It turns out the infertility experience from 1984 to 1992 was like training wheels for what was to come on May 12, 2014. The emotional roller-coaster ride that would come in waves over the next many months was overwhelming. Would my husband survive? If he survived, would he *live?* Would that life be Hell? When would I know how this was going to turn out? How would I know? What would it do to us? What would it do to the kids? What would it do to *me?*

As Bob moved from hospital, to rehab, to home, and recovery continued its slow, agonizing pace, there were certainly times I was miserable. But it was misery born of exhaustion and frustration, not of unhappiness. Yes, I still sometimes mourn the loss of the life we'd had together. There are times I feel sorry for myself and envy the ease with which our friends can move about, go places, and do things. But I wouldn't characterize it as unhappiness.

From the onset I decided that this experience, whatever was to come, would not ruin my life but enrich it, make me stronger, make me better. I was going to own this thing, and I was going to do everything I could to make sure my husband came out of it as whole as possible. I would take comfort in that, and that comfort and satisfaction would sustain me no matter what happened. I would enjoy the time with him, because each day with him was a gift. And I would ask him to forgive me every time I lost my patience or had trouble dealing with the demands of his care.

About eleven months into his recovery, Bob and I attended a booster club Beef 'n' Beer for the high school baseball team. Bob was on the coaching staff, having returned to his position coaching the freshmen, which he had done the previous two years. He had ended the 2014 season in a Virginia ICU, missing his team's last game. When he had contacted the varsity head coach and athletic director in February 2015—still in rehab and still in a wheelchair—and told them he wanted to get back to coaching the freshman team in the spring, they and the booster club parents had been behind him all the way. At this event, after getting a full update on how Bob was doing, one of the parents asked me how *I* was doing. "Great!" I beamed. He looked at me in astonishment and with a great deal of skepticism. But I meant it. I knew he was skeptical, and so I quickly added that yes, of course it was hard, and some days were not so good, but in the grand scheme of things I really was doing great. I was having a beer and eating Italian food, surrounded by people who shared a love of baseball and admired my husband. What could be better? That night, with assistance, Bob had walked into the same restaurant that just four months earlier he'd had to be carried into by wheelchair. And he wasn't just a spectator, he was one of the coaches. I couldn't have been happier.

Strategy 3: Compartmentalize

> *Your ability to compartmentalize, prioritize, and focus enough time on each area in order to make incremental progress towards a conclusion will be your most important skill set to achieve significant success. Open, focus, then close the compartment.*
>
> —Ryan Blair, author and entrepreneur

My boss at the time of the stroke told me later that he was very impressed with how I was able to compartmentalize my life in those early weeks. I did not realize it at the time, but it is exactly what I did, and it was one of the key strategies that helped me not only to cope emotionally but to manage everything. Taking care of Bob meant more than visiting him and consulting with the doctors. It meant having a family income and health insurance. It meant hanging onto the new job I had just started the week earlier. I did not yet qualify for family leave, and I had no earned time off. Bob had no income and no disability pay as a self-employed businessman. I also had our children, both of whom were in college, who needed me to provide stability. I had the house to maintain and Bob's business to keep intact, if not fully operating. Thankfully, my company had a policy that allowed me to borrow from my personal time off. My job was already set up to be done remotely from my home office, so I took off the first four days after Bob's stroke and surgery but the next week scheduled my days to work from the hotel. I knew I would need time off later on if he survived the first month, so I had to be judicious in what I spent. And I had to keep working.

I had been offered a house to stay in that was about twenty minutes from the hospital, so for the rest of the time in Virginia I worked a daily routine of 8:00 a.m. to 6:00 p.m. from the makeshift office where I was staying, with 12:00 p.m. until 2:00 p.m. reserved for Bob and doctors' consults. Evenings were for phone calls with friends and family; weekends were for more visits with Bob, household/partner business, and the kids. Bob was in a coma for most of that time, but it was important to me that I was there, in case he could hear anything. A lunchtime routine gave me access to the doctors as they did their rounds. And I avoided the rush-hour beltway traffic, so less of the two hours was spent in the car. Because I knew I was going to spend at least a full hour with Bob, I could give my job the attention it needed from eight to twelve and two to six. It gave me structure so I could focus, and for a short time it was my "normal."

As time went on and the situation changed, I established new normals. It has been a constant of new normals as Bob has transitioned from hospital, to skilled nursing, to rehab, home, and beyond. I expect the new normals will continue for as long as Bob continues to progress.

Strategy 4: Take care of yourself

In dealing with those who are undergoing great suffering, if you feel burnout setting in, if you feel demoralized and exhausted, it is best, for the sake of everyone, to withdraw and restore yourself. The point is to have a long term perspective.

—Dalai Lama, spiritual leader

What does it mean, exactly, to take care of yourself in times of crisis? In baseball terms, I knew that I was suddenly both catcher and backstop for Team Bucceri. So the first thing it meant to me was that I had to pace myself. I started with the standard checklist: eat a healthy diet, get plenty of rest, exercise, keep my own medical checkups. The only ones I really did with any regularity were eat well, rest, and maintain my medical checkups. Sleep was elusive, so despite my attempts to prevent it, sleep deprivation was a major enemy. But I made sure I at least rested. I did not need an alarm clock. On the rare days I slept in a little bit, I let myself. But I did use stairs, walked as much as possible, and did some mild stretching. About a year prior I had started a therapeutic massage program to help me manage chronic neck pain. I kept up with that for the first few months. It became more difficult once Bob came home and I could not leave him alone, so it became an occasional thing I did when the kids were around. But it would be a full fourteen months before I would start back to any regular workout program.

I discovered quickly that if I looked pulled together on the outside I felt pulled together on the inside, and that became my morning routine. So, checklist aside, taking care of myself in the early days meant keeping up appearances and looking put together even in casual clothes; getting my nails done a few times; remembering the makeup, even if it was just a little lipstick and mascara; keeping my hair appointments; and allowing myself to enjoy a glass of wine with dinner. Maybe a vodka and tonic before dinner. Okay, sometimes maybe two.

I did maintain some social life while Bob was in the hospital. During the summer months I went to a movie, a couple of our season ticket minor league baseball games, and a girls' night out, and I made lots of phone calls. I am not sure I could have coped as well without the friendships that came with those outings and calls.

Once Bob got home, I became determined to maintain a social life for the two of us and occasionally manage time out for myself with my friends. The latter was harder to do, because for the first year and a half it required arranging caregiver support if neither of our children were around. We were already spending Bob's retirement money on the caregiver during the workweek, and he was tired of caregivers by the time weekends rolled around, so finding alone time for me was very hard during the first eighteen months when he could not be left alone. But eventually, with the lifeline of a medical alert pendant around his neck, he achieved enough independence to be left alone for a few hours at a time.

Strategy 5: Take one day at a time

"It is a mistake to try to look too far ahead. The chain of destiny can only be grasped one link at a time."

—Winston S. Churchill Prime Minister of the United Kingdom, 1940-1945, 1951-1955

I learned quickly that I was going to have to let go of my tendency to look ahead and plan. In the first days of Bob's hospitalization, the doctors made it clear that I could not make any plans. "We're just going for survival," the ICU doctor said to me. It was like getting hit between the eyes with a hammer. It was pointless to try to set any expectations as to when Bob would start to wake up, what a recovery plan might look like, or when he'd move to rehab. There was a good chance none of those things would even happen. The twenty-four hour mortality rate is 75 percent, and the thirty-day mortality rate for his type of brain injury is 40–80 percent. It took me a long time to accept that. If he did survive, it would only become clear slowly over time how much function he'd ever recover. "What do I tell my employer?" I asked the doctors. They had no answer for me, because they really did not know.

This uncertainty did not change even at the seven-month mark. While mortality was no longer the concern, the therapists could not give us any indication of how far Bob's recovery would or could go. Despite all the months and all the progress, they still could not tell us whether Bob would ever walk under his own power again, whether the arm and shoulder issues would be resolved, or whether he would ever use the arm at all. All they would say was that he was responding well, progressing well, and they thought they could help him achieve his goals. But no certainties and no time frame were ever indicated. The unspoken message was this could take years if it happened at all.

So how do you deal with that? We live in a society that requires planning. I had to plan, even if it was to plan how to get through this without a plan. I am not kidding. Initially I made plans a week at a time. The first week's plan was to stay within walking distance of the hospital, so that we could get some rest but be there within minutes if Bob took a turn for the worse. The second week it was to settle in a mile down the road and put in the work time but still be able to get to the hospital quickly if Bob took a turn for the worse—and so on.

Eventually I made plans a month out, assessed them weekly and reserved the right to alter the plans at any moment. I became good at having a contingency plan, and the truth is I trained myself to just let the plans happen or not happen and not get all worked up if they didn't. The best example was my professional association's fortieth anniversary gala event. I was on the board of directors, and both Bob and I really wanted to go, but as events unfolded, it was being held just forty-eight hours after Bob was discharged from his surgery. He had not been home in over five months.

I paid the one hundred and twenty-five dollars for the tickets, but I had no idea whether we would go. The day of the event we still didn't know, but we kept our day quiet on the off chance that we'd feel up to it. I knew Bob wanted to go and get out in the world. I knew he wanted to wear something besides sweat pants for a change. But we didn't decide until four in the afternoon, when it was time to dress.

It was a good decision. Bob enjoyed being out with business people, listening to the keynote speaker, meeting my colleagues, and wearing a suit and dress shoes. It was not without its mishaps. In fact, we almost ended up on the pavement in the parking lot after the event. It was dark, and we were at the far end of the parking lot, because we did not yet have a handicapped placard for the car. Instead of turning his backside to the car and sitting on the seat, as we had trained, he attempted to step into the car. I couldn't see what had gone wrong, so it was all I could do to keep us from collapsing on the ground. That gaffe aside, it was pretty good given where we were at that point.

I forgot my own strategy when it came time to plan the trip to Florida. I waited until about a week and a half out to buy the plane tickets but bought nonrefundable tickets out of habit. It all worked out in the end, but the truth is we were not sure we were really going to Florida until a couple of days before the scheduled flight.

Strategy 6: Don't just accept help, get help

Be brave enough to accept the help of others.

—Melba Cosgrove, PhD, author

I have always been a very independent person, but from the moment I got the call in Texas I knew I was ill prepared to handle whatever was hitting us. I also knew it was going to be up to me to get us through it. I needed someone, which turned out to be my new employer, to help me find a flight. The human resources director stayed in communication with me all through the night to find flights that would get me back east and through the next morning to make sure I made it to Washington okay. That was just the beginning. When my good friend Nancy brought up the idea of driving Ben to Virginia I initially said no, not wanting to put that burden on her. She'd already put in a full day of work at her demanding corporate job and she'd have to give up a night of sleep plus take unplanned time off the next day. I could not bring myself to ask her to do that, but when I touched base with her an hour later, she was no longer asking me, she was telling me. And I was so relieved.

What Nancy did for us that night was unforgettable. She provided comfort and support to our two children as they faced the very real possibility of losing their father and dealing with it on their own. It was comforting to me to know Nancy would be there with both kids in case anything happened before I got there.

I cannot list all the things that family members, friends, and even casual acquaintances did in the initial days and over many months to help our family cope and help Bob recover: the visits to Bob to keep up his morale, the dinners, the cards, the text messages, emails, phone calls, invitations to just take a break, the home safety modifications—even the weeding of flower beds! You name it and people came up with it. Bob and I decided to accept it all, even when it felt like too much and even if it felt awkward. (Did I really let someone weed the gardens?)

Our friends even went so far as to establish a recovery fund for Bob that was set up as a raffle. Bob and I had never accepted money from anyone except our parents, and even that had usually been loans—hell, some had even been at market interest rates! It was a little hard to wrap my head around it, but I knew the financial resources needed for Bob's recovery were going to be huge, even after the insurance issue was resolved, and we would need them over a long time. The friends who approached us convinced us it was okay to accept help.

We also accepted help in the form of counseling. While an inpatient, Bob participated in psychotherapy, and periodically I would join him. During one of our sessions, we were seemingly chatting when the therapist asked us if we had ever been annoyed with each other in our thirty-two years of marriage. I don't recall what prompted her to ask it, but we looked at each other, burst out laughing, and cried out, "Hell, yes!" She then told us that while everything in our lives had changed with Bob's stroke on May 12, that part of our life had not. In a sense, she gave us permission to get annoyed, get mad—to be ourselves. She said I did not have to walk on eggshells around Bob, nor did he with me. It was something I needed to hear.

Months later, when we were home, learning how to live together under those difficult circumstances, I would remember what the therapist had said. We did bark. We did get annoyed with each other. Bob would alternately accuse me of pushing him too hard and not letting him do things. I'd get frustrated with my new role as full-time caregiver and the demands of having to immediately respond to every need. When would I get to be a wife again? When would I get time for me that didn't require major planning, money, or help from others? There were no answers to those questions, but therapy that provided practical, actionable help was invaluable to me.

Strategy 7: Do your homework

"Knowledge is power. Information is liberating. Education is the premise of progress, in every society, in every family.

—Kofi Annan, Secretary-General of the United Nations, 1997-2006

When the insurance company kept denying the referrals to acute rehab, I quickly contacted our family lawyer to find out whether I had any legal recourse. He referred me to a patient advocacy firm, and when their efforts did not seem to be having an impact, they referred me to another legal firm. I trusted the referrals, but the truth was that neither the advocate nor the attorney seemed to understand the laws that govern employer-based health plans and appeals.

I spent a big chunk of our savings on advocacy and legal fees to make sure I had experts help me get Bob the rehab he needed. I needed to keep working to pay the bills, so I felt I had no choice but to seek help. I had no confidence that the appeals process controlled by the insurance industry would work in Bob's favor, and I did not want him languishing in a nursing home any longer than he had to. I'd heard too many stories of lengthy battles that came down on the patient's side too late to make a difference, so I don't entirely regret the decision to hire an advocate or attorney before exhausting the appeals process. But I learned late in the process that I was paying for some on-the-job training because they really did not understand how healthcare is governed.

In hindsight, I realize that with just a little more homework I might have saved some money by finding a law firm that was already familiar with employer-based health plans and ERISA. ERISA is the Employee Retirement Income Security Act of 1974, a major US law that guarantees pensions to certain categories of employees after a certain period with their employers.[2] It is also the law that includes the rules governing employer-based health plans, which is *our* health plan. What I unfortunately paid a lawyer one hundred and fifty dollars an hour to learn for me is the following:

1. The health insurance company's internal and external appeals process must be exhausted before legal action can be taken.

2. If a patient loses on external appeal, he or his advocate can file the case in a federal court, but there is no jury and no face-to-face testimony. A judge decides the case based on review of the documentation related to the case. The patient or advocate could submit a written affidavit, but that would be it.

3. Awards are limited to the benefit. This means that if the patient dies there is no claim against the health plan, because there is no one to receive the benefit. There is no apparent accountability to the health plan should the patient die because they could not get the services covered under the denied benefit. Remember when Bob fell at the nursing home and opened a wound on his head? I now understand what the nurse manager meant when she said he "had the right to fall." If he had died as a result of that fall, I don't believe I would have had any luck with a negligence lawsuit nor do I believe I would have been able to sue the insurance company for keeping him in a facility that could not keep him safe.

---

[2] https://www.dol.gov/general/topic/retirement/erisa.

4. The patient or his advocate can ask the court to order the health plan to reimburse the patient for the out-of-pocket legal expenses incurred as a result of the denied benefit, but there is no guarantee that such an award will be granted, and there is no provision for pain and suffering.

I am not a legal expert, and the above observations cannot be construed as legal opinion, but I include them here to raise awareness of how the federal laws that govern the health care system do not tend to favor the patient or member, no matter how the law is titled. It is very important to do enough homework about what laws govern the health plan involved in the denial and then, if you need an advocate or attorney, hire one who has experience with those laws.

Strategy 8: Maintain a sense of humor

Laugh as much as possible, always laugh. It's the sweetest thing one can do for oneself and one's fellow human beings.

—Maya Angelou, poet

Find *something* **to laugh about,** especially in your darkest moment. Humor is life's anesthesia to its pain. When my father was dying in 2006, he called me over to his gurney right before the doctors wheeled him into emergency surgery to remove his gallbladder. I eagerly went to his side, knowing these might be his last words and hoping for some new declaration of his love for me. He took my hand, looked up at me, and whispered, "Don't forget to pay the taxes." He then told me what to do. To this day I love telling that story, because it makes me laugh and remember my father fondly even in his darkest hour. It was so like my father to show his love by being Mr. Business and taking care of practical things to the bitter end.

Bob has a great sense of humor, and it is one of the things that made me fall in love with him all those years ago. At my college graduation my father stood by Bob, my then fiancé, and wondered out loud what the hell I could do with a degree in philosophy. After a thoughtful moment, Bob quipped, "Be a shepherd?" It made my dad laugh out loud, which none of my prior boyfriends had ever managed to do, and it endeared Bob to my dad from that day forward.

There is nothing funny about what happened that night in May, yet there was something almost comical in my attempt to get to the airport. Somehow I got the newest cabbie in the Dallas-Fort Worth area. He kept driving by the hotel, looking for us, and we could see him going up and down the boulevard. My boss was jumping up and down in the parking lot, screaming into his phone and waving frantically as he tried to get the cabbie's attention. "Over here, man! O, come on—are you kidding me? We're right here!" After finally finding us right in front of his nose and picking me up, the driver, who was clearly from the Middle East, kept making small talk about how he was also from Philadelphia and loved cheese steak. He overshot the airport *three* times, despite the huge signs with big arrows that clearly said "DFW Airport THIS WAY." I ended up taking over and directing his every turn, all one of them. Of course, all this cost me the flight I was trying to catch, but he smiled proudly because he'd actually got me to my destination—and asked me for a tip. I almost burst out laughing at the absurdity of it all. I felt as if I were living a Coen brothers' movie. I found a couple of bucks and slapped them into his hand, hoping he'd be insulted, but he wasn't. I think he thought he had done a great job.

I especially noticed how important humor was those times when I lost sight of it. And that still does happen from time to time. The first week Bob was home was particularly hard because neither one of us was sleeping, and the physical work of helping him get around and carry out the activities of daily living was brutal on me.

As much as I had prepared for his return, I was not prepared for the physical demands. My every muscle and nerve ached, and I was completely exhausted from sleep deprivation. For a time, that was all I could think of. At some point I realized that I had completely lost my sense of humor, and it was grinding me down to a nub. I was going to die wheeling Bob down the hall to use the bathroom, I just knew it!

I have to confess I am not sure what it was that helped me get it back. It might have been Bob and something he said. Maybe it wasn't even funny but touching and just enough to make me tell myself to lighten up already. He has a way of saying things that either melt my heart or just make me laugh. Like the time he was experiencing bladder challenges, when he looked up at me proudly from the toilet at the sound of his long-anticipated pee. "Hear that?" he said. "I sound like Secretariat!" I burst out laughing.

A former colleague whom I had lost touch with over the years contacted me after she heard about Bob. This was around the seventh month. She wanted to offer herself up as a resource to me, knowing how hard it is to find someone who can truly relate. Her fifty-five-year-old husband had been diagnosed with ALS two and a half years earlier. When she shared with me how good her teenage sons were with their father and how they could make light of something involving him or tease him even as they were transferring him in a Hoyer lift, I burst into tears. I was so moved by what she told me. I was grateful for her and for the gift her sons had—the gift to ease her pain and their father's pain with gentle humor. Whatever you do, find something to laugh about.

Strategy 9: Forgive yourself

> *The Christian life is not a constant high. I have my moments of deep discouragement. I have to go to God in prayer with tears in my eyes, and say, "O God, forgive me," or "Help me."*

—the Reverend Billy Graham, evangelist

I know how much I love Bob and he loves me. He is my soul mate and best friend. But going from wife and lover to full-time caregiver in an instant and facing the prospect that the caregiver role may never go away has tested me to my very core. I have not always been pleasant. There have been moments of impatience. I have even sometimes felt resentful at the loss of autonomy.

Some days I am the perfect vision of patient and doting wife. Some days I am not. One night I uncharacteristically said something that stung Bob. I don't remember exactly what I said, but it was sarcastic. I acknowledged my bad behavior, apologized, and told him I hated myself at that moment for having said it. "I stink at this," I said. We cried together as he forgave me and apologized for putting me through it all.

During Lent, our parish priest informed us that confessions the Saturday before Holy week would go from three o'clock until five o'clock in the afternoon. I leaned over to Bob and whispered, "We'd better get here early. I have a lot to confess." It made us both laugh.

Later in the year, I was trying to do a small home repair and failing miserably. It was the kind of thing too small to hire someone to do. No one would even want the job, and it looked easy. The package showed a woman in June Cleaver dress and heels doing the job effortlessly! After creating a mess, throwing away what I'd just bought at the hardware store, and cursing up a storm, I collapsed on the bed in tears. Bob knew to just leave me alone for a while.

I know that kind of behavior hurts him. But he forgave me, as he always does. And I forgave me, too. I know I am doing the best I can.

Bob knows I would be lost without him, and I frequently tell him so and ask him to try to remember that next time I act like a raving lunatic.

Strategy 10: Semper avanti—always look forward

There are far, far, better things ahead than any we leave behind.

—C. S. Lewis, author

Probably the most important strategy that both Bob and I have used throughout this whole experience was to always look forward and never look back. To the best of my knowledge, Bob has spent every waking moment focused on moving ahead, to regain the use of his leg, arm, and cognitive skills. He has never wallowed in self-pity. He has never cried and asked why this happened to him. Neither have I. I've never seen the point. From the moment I got that phone call, I've kept moving forward. As I saw it then and see it now, the only way out of such a situation is to work our way out one step, one day, one milestone at a time.

As Bob survived and reached each milestone, it became increasingly important to make sure he was given the opportunity to reach the next one. When I learned that only about 20 percent of people who suffer his kind of injury recover their function enough to live independently, I decided he would be in the 20 percent until he proved he was not.

I adopted "Semper avanti" as my rallying cry very early on. I got the phrase from the mother of the man whose house I stayed in when Bob was in Virginia. The man is Bob's client, and his mother befriended me, almost adopting me as a surrogate daughter. She is a devout Catholic who has her own story to tell, of nursing her late husband through his decline and eventual passing. She knew a thing or two about how to survive personal crisis. And she told me it was always important to just keep moving forward. "Nancy, just remember: Semper avanti," she'd say when I'd tell her the latest news from the doctors. I liked it, and so I started signing off with it as I wrote my blog. Whether it was to pick me up after a setback or to celebrate a victory, it was my way of telling our family and friends, near and far, that we were still in this thing.

Epilogue

Bob marked the one-year anniversary of his stroke by speaking to a crowd of sixty health information technology professionals about his experience and his fight to recover his former life. While Ben had to work that night, Julia was able to attend with us. Bob wrote his own speech and spoke eloquently about what it had been like to wake up in a hospital completely unaware of what had happened. He described how it had taken months before the enormity of his stroke had sunk in. He spoke about not looking back, about being scared but forging ahead and listening to his body and his inner voice. He talked about the importance of weaving work and coaching back into his day along with the therapy exercises. He called to mind his hero, Lou Gehrig, and how Gehrig had battled the ravages of ALS.

I spoke about the challenge of navigating the health care system as Bob transitioned from one place to the next and the failure of the electronic health record systems to enable information to follow him as he went. I spoke of how I believed the poor communication and lack of accurate, timely information contributed to the problem I had getting Bob into acute rehab from Virginia, and I related the various communication problems we experienced throughout the five-months Bob was being cared for. He had been in three hospitals, a skilled nursing facility, and an acute inpatient rehab hospital in three health systems across two disconnected states.

The duplicate procedures, extra hospitalizations, and rescheduled tests contributed not only unnecessary cost to Bob's care but stress and inconvenience to us as a family.

We called our talk "Trouble with the Curve," and it was a fitting event to be held before a Phillies-Pirates baseball game. Here are his remarks in their entirety.

Trouble with the Curve
(Address to the Delaware Valley chapter of the Healthcare Information and Management Systems Society, Citizen's Bank Park, Philadelphia, Pennsylvania)

Having the stroke is just half the story. The other half is the stages of recovery. You wake up in a hospital, and you don't know what happened, how you got there. I don't remember much about the few days leading up to the stroke, because it was all routine stuff.

It takes about three months before you realize what is going on, how serious the injury was. People tell you your arm was affected, but you don't know what that means.

In my case it meant severe subluxation of the shoulder and a continual stiffening and curling of the fingers, which has made the arm unusable.

The most important thing you have to do is move forward. About eight weeks in, the psychologist met with me for the first time, asked me if I knew what had happened to me, and asked me if I wanted to know more about it.

I think she liked my answer, because she smiled when I said, "Not really. I am more interested in focusing on going forward than looking behind me."

So where am I now? It's important not to be scared and to push yourself to find your limits. If you don't do that, you won't reach your full potential. Listen to your body and listen to your therapists, because they'll tell you different stories.

For example, on New Year's Day I went for a long walk with my wife. It was hard, exhausting, and I was yelled at by my therapist for taking such risks. But I tell you, after that walk I never felt better, and I'd do it again in a heartbeat.

The therapists were skeptical and looked at me a little like I was nuts, but I went back to coaching high school baseball this spring. Yes, from a wheelchair. It's been an important step in recovering my life. I have been a baseball coach on and off for thirty years. But I think it has also been good for my players, who have been great about having a coach in a wheelchair.

One of my role models has always been Lou Gehrig, so maybe I got my inspiration from him. In his final full season with the New York Yankees, while [he was] suffering from the effects of ALS, his wife had to dress him in his uniform at their apartment and put him in a cab to Yankee Stadium.

Eleanor would then call the Yankee Clubhouse to say Lou was on his way. At the stadium, two teammates would meet the cab and bring him into the clubhouse. Despite requiring so much care, he still had a batting average close to .300. Not many players have that in their prime, let alone when being ravaged by ALS. He also was an American League All-Star that year.

What I lack in mobility I make up for in experience. For example, I talked my other coach into putting all of our subs in a tied game. We have sixteen players.

Before players go up to bat I like to talk to them about what to expect from the pitcher. Hitting is largely confidence. Baseball is a team sport, but a lot of it is done alone. I try to give a player some insight into what to expect before stepping into the batter's box so he goes in with some confidence.

One of the subs drew a walk and keyed the rally for us. The next sub got a hit, which drove in the first two runs of the winning rally.

And I am getting back into my business with small jobs, such as writing a short decision paper on proposed legislation on electronic benefits transfer in Kansas.

I do best by doing real things. The therapists have games and puzzles, and I do them. But I was editing a technical document before I even got into acute rehab. I did better at that than puzzles.

Do real things, things that accomplish something or have meaning in your life.

Nancy and I went down to Wilmington last week to see a minor league baseball game. Sitting in the box next to us was one of my players, a kid named Travis. When a foul ball was hit into the stands near us, he joined the scrum of other kids chasing down the treasured ball. As luck would have it, Travis came away with the ball. Then he came over to us with the ball and said, "Coach, this is for you."

As a baseball coach I have buckets of balls, but none as valuable as this one.

Thank you for your attention and allowing us to share our story. Now, down to the field for some baseball!

Bob completed his third season of coaching the freshman baseball team at West Chester East High School, with strong support from his coaching colleagues, booster club, and—most endearing—his players. He coached from his wheelchair, and he loved it, although it killed him that he couldn't run out on the field, take them through their stretches and throw batting practice. I started the season concerned that Bob would be accommodated out of a sense of loyalty but regarded as inconsequential. He needed another coach to serve as arms and legs and to serve as administrator while he continued his recovery. Would he be able to retain the respect he had earned over his thirty-year span of coaching? Would he earn the respect of the new players and parents and of his fellow coach?

Despite his lack of mobility, Bob's experience was an asset to the team. This was reaffirmed a year later when Bob was invited to attend the 2016 annual banquet. Bob had decided to retire from coaching so he could focus on his business. But the boys that had been his first freshman team were now graduating, so he attended their final home game and was invited to come to the banquet.

We had a great time at the banquet just being there. But we were both completely blown away at the end when, out of the blue, Bob was called to the podium by the senior players to receive recognition for his role in getting them started in their baseball careers. The spokesman for the senior players was a young man named Ryan. He spoke eloquently about how Bob was the first coach that wasn't their dad, or their friend's dad. He was a "real" coach, and taught them how to be high school baseball players. He talked about what Bob taught them that year, and then what Bob continued to teach them, referring to the mile walk Bob had recently completed. "Next time I see you, Coach, I want to hear it was two". I laughed to myself as I thought, "Wow, now who's coaching who?"

Bob's progress continues slowly but surely. He continues to progress with his walking, and has set a goal of running again. He is relearning his computer skills.

I continue to have mostly good but some bad days, days when I am so happy and grateful for what I have and others when I mourn the loss of what we had together and struggle in my role as twenty-four-hour caregiver. I am still catcher and backstop, and some days it is daunting. I try not to think about all the plans we'd made for our empty-nest years and the things we can't do. In many ways it has been a wonderful and rewarding journey, and I try to stay focused on those things that made it so.

I look to what we can do that maybe we never would have thought to do—like go to a rock concert. We never go to rock concerts. But on June 20, 2015, we took a road trip to Pittsburgh and with our twenty-two-year-old daughter saw the Rolling Stones. It was a night we will never forget. It rained. In fact, it poured all through the warm-up band. But within minutes of the Stones taking the stage, the rain stopped and a rainbow arced over Heinz Field. "Look at that," said Bob from under one of my old ponchos from my Girl Scout years. "God's a Rolling Stones fan!" Within the first hour, Bob was standing, and he stayed that way for the rest of the concert, not missing a thing.

Eighteen months after the stroke, I escorted Bob to the seventeenth annual EBT Next Generation conference in Phoenix, Arizona. He refused to use a wheelchair and walked the entire conference center and exhibit hall on his own. He marked his return by moderating a ninety-minute panel, Front Page Focus, in front of 340 people, standing strong at the podium and engaging the panel of executives and federal officials in lively discussion on topical issues affecting the EBT industry.

I don't know what the future holds—how far Bob's recovery will take him, what lies ahead for either of us professionally, how well our children will continue to grow and thrive as they enter adulthood, or what other challenges lie around the corner. I'll deal with it when it happens. And through it all I will strive to cherish each day, make every one count, see the blessings in my life, and always, always look forward. Semper avanti.

Bob and Nancy joining in on Red Nose Day, May 21,
2015. Whatever you do, remember to laugh!

Printed in the United States
By Bookmasters